"Aren't you glad you worship a God of grace? Tim Kimmel has done a great job of reminding us as parents that we are the model of God in our home and we need to be good grace-based parents."

—Dr. Kevin Leman
Author of *Making Children Mind Without Losing Yours* and *First-Time Mom*

"You're about to enter a much needed 'No Guilt Zone' when it comes to parenting advice. It's the very place you want to be if your heart's desire is to raise loving, honoring, creative, expressive kids — secure enough to stand against the "crowd" because they're secure enough in their faith and themselves. For over twenty years, we've peaked inside the Kimmel home, seen grace-based parenting lived out in the lives of their outstanding children, and applied many of these principles with our own children. We think this book will be a bestseller because it's a unique, fresh, freeing look at what really works in bringing out the best in you and your child. In fact, get two copies because you're going to want to give one to a friend."

—John and Cindy Trent
Authors, speakers, president of StrongFamilies.com

"I have seen firsthand that Tim Kimmel is not just a highly-skilled communicator, he is a deeply devoted dad. Put those two together, and you have the right man with the right message. Read this if you want to be equipped for life's greatest and most challenging task."

—John Ortberg

"If parenting were on a payroll, it would qualify for hazardous duty. While there has always been a disconnect between generations in lifestyle, the twenty-first century parent needs the nerves of a test pilot and the patience of a brooding hen to steer children wisely. Probably no other occupation commands such a high level of commitment riding on a lifetime of impact. Few writers are as well equipped as Tim Kimmel to teach parents how to fan flames of youthful self-determination and at the same time avoid self-destruction. His longtime parental and pastoral experience thrusts his readers into the hottest contemporary issues and offers a cool anxiety-damper. *Grace-Based Parenting* tames the family inferno with biblical know-how—a spiritual fire extinguisher for young Christian families."

—Howard G. Hendricks

"Dr. Tim Kimmel is America's Parenting expert! Don't we all want to raise healthy, solid kids that love God and love us? Sure we do! *Grace-Based Parenting* is a hands-on road map for parents who need a sure-fire guarantee in raising kids to become healthy adults. Tim has developed these principles over a lifetime. They are clear, articulate and show a pathway of raising our kids the way God raises us…through grace."

—Dr. Gary and Barbara Rosberg
Hosts of America's Family Coaches-Live! Speakers, authors and founders of
Divorce Proofing America's Marriages Campaign

"Grace-Based Parenting will help parents produce a new generation of young people who are driven to be used of God in powerful ways because of the profound sense of love, purpose, and hope that they have at the core of their being."

—Josh McDowell
Author and speaker

"Grace-Based Parenting is a liberating, life changing book for parents who want to give a legacy of faith to their children. Parenting God's way is the pathway of grace and Tim Kimmel gives guidance, which will produce tremendous kids and families which honor and serve the Lord Jesus Christ."

—Dr. Jack Graham
Pastor, Prestonwood Baptist Church
President, Southern Baptist Convention

"Tim Kimmel is a master of the wild and wooly world of parenting. He has been a light to my family reminding us that of all things to remember and to embrace— Parents and children are equally in need of the glorious grace of God. Tim and Darcy are amazing parents—sweet and strong and kind and bold. They write with humor, hope, and an honesty that allows us all to let down our guard and allow God to meet us in our fears and regrets. This superb book will invite you to see the privilege we have as parents to be conformed to Christ through our own children."

—Dan B. Allender, Ph.D.
President, Mars Hill Graduate School
Author of *The Wounded Heart* and *How Children Raise Parents*

"Tim's wonderful wisdom and wit come together in this book to help all of us parent-types (and grandparent-types) get through the deep weeds of parenting with rich and workable insights."

—Dr. Joseph M. Stowell
President, Moody Bible Institute

GRACE
BASED
PARENTING

OTHER RESOURCES BY DR. TIM KIMMEL

BOOKS:

Little House on the Freeway
Raising Kids Who Turn Out Right
Homegrown Heroes
How to Deal With Powerful Personalities
Basic Training for a Few Good Men

VIDEO STUDIES FOR SMALL GROUPS AND CHURCHES:

The Hurried Family Video Series
Raising Kids Who Turn Out Right Video Series
Basic Training for a Few Good Men Video Series
Grandparenthood: More Than Rocking Chairs

Dr. Tim Kimmel does keynote speaking and also conducts
parenting, marriage, and men's conferences throughout the
United States.

To obtain any of these resources
or to contact Dr. Kimmel:

Family Matters™
P.O. Box 14382
Scottsdale, AZ 85267-4382

www.familymatters.net
800-467-4596

GRACE BASED PARENTING

Set Your Family Free

DR. TIM KIMMEL

W PUBLISHING GROUP™

www.wpublishinggroup.com

A Division of Thomas Nelson, Inc.
www.ThomasNelson.com

Published by W Publishing Group, a division of Thomas Nelson, Inc., P.O. Box 141000, Nashville, Tennessee 37214.

Unless otherwise indicated, Scripture quotations used in this book are from the Holy Bible, New International Version®. Copyright © 1973, 1978, 1984, International Bible Society. Used by permission of Zondervan Bible Publishers.

Other Scripture references are from the following sources:

The Holy Bible, New Century Version® (NCV). Copyright © 1987, 1988, 1991 by Word Publishing, a Division of Thomas Nelson, Inc. Used by permission. All rights reserved.

The New King James Version (NKJV®). Copyright © 1979, 1980, 1982 by Thomas Nelson Publishers, Inc.

New American Standard Bible (NASB), © 1960, 1977 by the Lockman Foundation.

Library of Congress Cataloging-in-Publication Data

Kimmel, Tim.
    Grace-based parenting / by Tim Kimmel.
      p. cm.
    ISBN 0-8499-1803-0
    1. Parenting—Religious aspects—Christianity. 2. Grace (Theology). I. Title.
BV4529.K55 2004
248.8'45—dc22   2003022194

Printed in the United States of America

03 04 05 06 07 BVG 9 8 7 6 5 4 3 2 1

Dedicated to my granddaughter,
Riley Grace Murray:
You are the incarnation of your mother's spirit
and the personification of your middle name.

contents

FOREWORD

It's a quick trip from playing "little piggies" with a toddler's toes to packing her up for college. And every step of the way, parents utter the universal prayer: "Father, help me love this child as you loved me. Help me get this parenting thing right."

We get advice from older parents. We listen to tapes. We read books. We want more than anything to honor God by helping our children grow up spiritually strong and secure in our love.

This book is an answer to that prayer, for Tim Kimmel is a dad gifted by God to help the rest of us "get it right." I've known and admired the Kimmel family for two decades. I've heard Tim speak, read what he's written, and learned from his thoughts. Most of all, I've seen the way he adores his wife and cherishes his kids.

Tim knows families. And he knows how to help ours. Tim helps us grasp what it is our children need most from us. And, just as importantly, he gives us practical, good-sense ways to give our children the security of unconditional, grace-filled love. In doing so, Tim helps us give our children the greatest gift: a heart that yearns for God.

Do yourself and your family a favor. Read this book.

—MAX LUCADO

acknowledgments

This book enjoyed a touch of grace from many dear people.

Steve and Cheryl Green—It's been almost a decade of friendship. Thanks for believing so much and leading so well.

The W Group—Each one of you. I'm honored to be part of your team.

Laura Kendall—The savvy editor. Thanks for your tireless commitment to great reads.

David Moberg, Susan Ligon, and Debbie Wickwire—The "Amen" section of this author's life. I appreciate the confidence you showed from the very beginning . . . in me and in this message.

Mike Yorkey—You've been a stalwart for families for so long. Thanks for the tummy tuck you did on the original manuscript.

Wendy Wood—A woman who won't settle for good when great is so much better. I appreciate the dusting and polishing you did on my words.

Mark Sweeney—Every messenger needs a champion. You saw the big idea first. May your future take you higher and higher.

Tim Roberts and Susanne Freyling—The gatekeepers of Family Matters. Thanks for the thorough way you kept the lights shining while I was preoccupied.

Steve and Barbara Uhlmann—Two people who understand the strength of a quiet place. Thanks for the keys and the magnetic passes that provided the solitude needed to write this book.

Max Lucado—A humble giant. Your words have given me hope. Your life has shown me grace.

Karis, Cody, Shiloh, and Colt—The four best reasons I know for wanting to come home every evening. Thanks for the patience you showed me when I was still trying to figure out what all of this was about.

Darcy—A soul mate for all seasons. When I need grace the most, I never have to look farther than your green eyes.

And thank You, Jesus—Because Your grace is so sufficient, our families can be set free.

CHAPTER 1

WHY WELL-MEANING PARENTING FALLS SHORT

Indulge me for a minute. This won't take long. I want to use a scenario to set the stage for our discussion about parenting.

For starters, I'll need you to pull up a chair on one of the sides of this card table I'm looking at. You'll notice that it is crowded with tiny pieces of an elaborate jigsaw puzzle. You can tell—just by looking at the colors and designs on the pieces—that this is going to be a bit of a challenge.

Before you tear into this project, though, there are a few things you need to know about what you're looking at:

→ The border pieces have all been removed. I know it's easier to start a jigsaw puzzle by putting the edge pieces together to form a border. That gives you an early sense of accomplishment before you move on to the difficult stuff. Sorry. You'll have to decide the boundaries of this puzzle for yourself.

→ Somebody threw a couple of handfuls of pieces from a *different* puzzle into the box. They may look like they belong to this one, but they don't. They won't fit no matter how hard you try. And because you don't know which ones they are, you could waste a lot of time before you find out.

Are you ready to start putting the puzzle together? I realize I've complicated matters for you, but you're fairly resourceful. Given enough time and enough soothing medication, you could probably figure it out. All you need is the picture on the box cover and you can begin.

Oh, I forgot to mention something: We lost the cover to the box. You're just going to have to guess what this picture puzzle is supposed to look like. Does this sound like fun? I can't speak for you, but I'd rather get my gums scraped. If anything, this puzzle project sounds more like a sick joke. It's tough enough when you have all the right pieces, all the edge pieces, and the picture on the box. Take those things away, and it's anybody's guess what you'll come up with. Not only that, but without a clear picture of what you are trying to put together, you'll never really know if you even came close to what it was supposed to be.

Welcome to the parenting puzzle

I have just described the job of raising children. You labor many years to put the right pieces all together, but when your children grow up, they often don't resemble what you thought you were creating. Even with the disappointments, however, raising children is still the greatest thing you'll ever do. It's greater than any milestone you can hit in your career. It dwarfs any fame you may receive for your ideas or your inventions. You've been handed a piece of history in advance—a gracious gift you send to a time you will not see—and you play the biggest role in how that history will ultimately be recorded. That's why, in spite of the challenges, you need to have a plan for parenting that works.

Good intentions aren't enough. Every parent starts out with them, but it doesn't take long before you find that you've been set up for failure by circumstances that you didn't plan on or ask for. Good parenting skills aren't enough either. You need something bigger than your brains and your wits to get you through.

Take the issue of boundaries. Just as the edge pieces of

> You've been handed a piece of history in advance—a gracious gift you send to a time you will not see.

the puzzle mentioned earlier were removed, our culture has removed many of the moral boundaries that made raising children more clear-cut. Right and wrong used to be black and white. Lying, cheating, stealing, and pushing your weight around at someone else's expense were wrong. Disrespect to people and property were obvious calls for parents to make.

We also had excellent guidelines to live by—like the Ten Commandments. But after decades of culture chipping away at them, the Ten Commandments are no longer etched deeply in stone but written in pencil on a Post-it note. They are more like ten hints or suggestions that you can use when it's in your best interest to do so. Somewhere along the way, they've lost their authority in the average family's life. To too many of today's parents, it is no longer "right and wrong" but what I *feel* is "right and wrong" that rules the day. This kind of thinking leads to two dangerous parenting extremes.

EXTREME PARENTS

One extreme consequence of erasing clear moral boundaries is a sense of taking license in some parents—even Christian parents. Their kids can hang out with whomever they choose, watch anything on television or at the movies that they'd like, act out their frustrations with little consequence, click on anything on the Internet that they'd like to see, start dating early, accommodate their sexual desires, and use whatever means works best for achieving success in school, sports, and relationships.

I said this is an *extreme* example. Most parents wouldn't admit to being in this category even if their names were Ozzy and Sharon Osborne. Regardless, somebody probably came to mind as you read those last few sentences. The local section of just about any daily newspaper reminds us that there are lots of parents who wield negative and even destructive influences on their children. They are guilty by either commission or omission of failing to lead their kids properly through childhood.

Unfortunately, even well-meaning parents can cave in to a certain degree to this type of parenting. It's actually quite easy to become a bit desensitized by the boundary-less culture we were raised in. We may do a noble job of leading our children when things are going well, but it's actually common for many of us to surrender some of our best convictions under duress. Our culture can be nasty and punitive to parents committed to doing the right thing. That's why so many parents acquiesce under stress. The painful reality is that too many parents would rather *feel* good than *do* good. Raising kids with clear moral boundaries can be an extremely lonely job. Who else in your neighborhood is trying to raise kids the way you are?

FROM ONE EXTREME TO THE OTHER

But there's another extreme that parents can go to that is equally toxic for children. In fact, it can leave scar tissue on their spiritual lives that may never go away. This form of parenting is often an overreaction to a life or a culture without boundaries. The extreme that I'm referring to is when parents bring the boundaries *in* far more tightly than they need to be to effectively raise their kids. These are parents who restrict or control just about everything. They tighten the boundaries regarding friends, entertainment, sports, education, and their spiritual lives, hoping that they have somehow made it *safer* for their children to go through life.

They haven't.

Some parents do this because that is how they were raised. The biggest candidates for this kind of extreme parenting, however, are those who were brought up in homes *without* boundaries. They often revert to this very controlling approach to parenting because they've seen how much damage can result when children are left to their own devices. These parents want to make sure their children don't become ensnared in the traps they found themselves in. And so to make certain that doesn't happen, they not only have clear moral boundaries, but they add inner fences to make it even more difficult for their children to get close to the edge. These parents are often driven to this strategy as a result of embracing two incorrect assumptions. First, they assume that their *obedience* to a stricter and tighter standard will somehow help them raise safer and better children.

It won't.

Since *how* children turn out is far more contingent on what is going on *inside them* than outside them, unnecessarily tight boundaries undermine the desire of the Holy Spirit, who is working to build a sense of moral resolve in their hearts.

The second incorrect assumption that drives parents to construct unnecessary inner fences around children is that it somehow helps them gain more favor or protection from God.

It doesn't. God can't give more of what He's already given in abundance when we become His children.

My parents were both brought up in homes where the moral boundaries were adjusted to fit the circumstances. Shortly after they were married, they both became Christians, which helped them realize that they didn't want to raise their children in the same kind of environment. They knew they needed to grow in their faith first, however, so they joined a church that would give them guidance in how they should live their lives and raise their children. Unfortunately, this particular church believed that the basic boundaries God outlined in the Scriptures needed more "development" and "clarification."

Take, for instance, the way church leaders handled the biblical concept of the "Sabbath," which Scripture says we are to keep "holy." Since "holy" meant "set apart," they wanted to make sure the Sabbath was as set apart from anything that looked like a normal day as possible. The church leaders defined the Sabbath as a day when you went to church and worshiped as a family (not a bad idea), and then went home and spent a quiet, restful afternoon (another idea that wasn't so bad). The pastor liked to elaborate on what both of these anchor tenets of a Sabbath Day looked like, and he taught these points as if they were inscribed on stone tablets themselves.

That's not all. "Worship" meant arriving on time, with *every* family member bringing their Bible (including infants, he said, "to get them in the habit"), *every* member of the family dropping some money in the offering plate, and then every family going straight home after church. Going out to restaurants with other families for lunch was discouraged. Once you were home, "rest and quiet" meant no television or radio (today he'd probably add "no computers"), no loud or active playing by the children, and nap times for everyone. You finished off the day by coming *back* to church for a junior version of what happened that morning.

It would have been fine if the pastor offered these as *suggestions* and encouraged my parents to confirm these through prayer. This would have allowed them to let God configure their Sabbath to meet its stated purpose in the Scriptures (to rest) in a way that aligned with the age and unique personalities of our family. But he didn't. This pastor taught his version of the Sabbath as the way "good" and "serious-minded" Christian families observed Sabbath. He also intimated that the church leaders had ways of checking up on members.

I'll never forget a time when I was seven years old. It was a perfect Sunday afternoon, light breeze and comfortable temps. I wasn't supposed to lie down until 3:00 p.m. Mom was cleaning up after lunch, and my other siblings had scattered to various corners of our house. I slipped outside with a rubber ball and began tossing it lightly against an outside wall of our brick house—a little game of catch with myself. I'd maybe thrown the ball a dozen times up against the wall when my mother came barreling out of the house.

"Tim, stop that immediately!"

"Why, Mom?"

"Because it's Sunday!"

"But Mom, why can't I play catch on Sunday?"

"We're not allowed to do things like that on Sunday."

"Who told you that?"

"God!"

Mom was so young in her relationship with God that she actually thought everything the pastor said was straight from God's mouth. And then she added the *coup de grâce*: "Besides, what if someone from the church drove by and saw you playing ball on Sunday?"

This statement points to a trap that some parents fall into when it comes to drawing tighter boundaries than what the Bible outlines: They often measure their effectiveness as parents by how they compare to others. They monitor other families and serve as a kind of "morals police," measuring these other parents' effectiveness by how well they meet their arbitrary and tighter standard. These parents have a knee-jerk reaction: They are often quick to stand in judgment if some other set of parents falls short. These parents are deluded into thinking that the families with children who learn to obey the most rules produce the best kids.

Hardly.

If anything, this is an excellent way to wreck your kids.

Fortunately, Mom figured out that she could increase her chances of raising great kids if she'd just lighten up. For her, God and some common sense worked just fine. Some of the best games of baseball I remember playing as a child were on Sunday afternoon, with my mom cheering me on. (By the way, that pastor started to "lighten up" himself once the little boys in his house became teenagers.)

Incidentally, all that I've just said doesn't preclude a stricter view of Sabbath rest. It simply changes the *reasons* why a family might choose to set aside one day a week to focus their attention on God. God could actually lead a family to observe one day of the week where quiet, rest, and minimal activity were the standards of the day. That could actually have a very beneficial impact on a busy, hurried family.

But it should be done out of a desire to focus on God and get rest rather than making the Bible say something that it doesn't and, in the process, practicing image control.

OUR WAY OR THE HIGHWAY

One of the things complicating the parenting puzzle is that even more pieces have been added to the picture than are necessary. These pieces don't actually fit into the picture, but they've been forced in because convincing voices insist that they belong there. These extra pieces don't necessarily have any power in determining the final image on our puzzle, but you wouldn't know that by the way they are presented. Strident voices tell parents that if they don't feed their children certain ways, or discipline them certain ways, or educate them certain ways, then they are setting their children up for certain doom. You can even infer from some of these teachings that God wouldn't be pleased if you tried to raise them outside these strict guidelines. Once again, it's one thing to offer these additional suggestions in these areas, but it's another thing to turn these suggestions into the *only* way to effectively parent children.

> Strident voices tell parents that if they don't feed their children certain ways, or discipline them certain ways, or educate them certain ways, then they are setting their children up for certain doom.

Like the voices at the drive-through windows of the world, the voices of some of these experts compel us to add things that aren't necessarily vital to effective parenting and clearly don't guarantee better results. I suppose it's fair to say that not one of these experts (at least that I've ever heard of) offering advice to parents claims that his or her method *guarantees* anything. Children are free agents and capable of resisting even the most effective parenting plans available. It's also fair to say that doing certain things as a parent obviously raises the odds that you will produce better kids—like having clearly defined moral boundaries. But within the clear boundaries of God's moral law in the Bible, there is actually a lot of latitude offered as to how to raise your children. Unfortunately, it's easy for some voices to frame many good ideas as *requirements* for effective parenting.

We're used to turning into the drive-through lane and hearing a chirpy voice say, "Do you want fries with that?" or "Would you like to supersize your order?" We hear a similar echo when we go looking for help in raising our children:

→ *I'm trying to figure out my options on feeding my new baby.* "Would you like breast-feeding with that?"

→ *I'm trying to figure out the best way to discipline my boy.* "Would you like spanking with that?"

→ *I'm trying to figure out how to educate my children.* "Would you like anything but public schooling with that?"

It's hard to maintain a balanced view of parenting when these voices are so loud and adamant. The proof that any model of parenting is effective is not how the parents and children get along. It isn't even in how well they treat and respect each other after they are all grown up. Even nonreligious families can accomplish this. The real test of a parenting model is how well equipped the children are to move into adulthood as vital members of the human race. Notice I didn't say "as vital members of the Christian community." We need to have kids that can be sent off to the most hostile universities, toil in the greediest work environments, and raise their families in the most hedonistic communities and yet not be the least bit intimidated by their surroundings. Furthermore, they need to be engaged in the lives of people in their culture, gracefully representing Christ's love inside these desperate surroundings. The apostle Paul gave us as parents an excellent goal for our children to pursue:

Do everything without complaining or arguing, so that you may become blameless and pure, children of God without fault in a crooked and depraved generation, in which *you shine like stars in the universe* as you hold out the word of life—in order that I may boast on the day of Christ that I did not run or labor for nothing. (Philippians 2:14–16, emphasis mine)[1]

Stepping back and looking at the product of the last generation and the direction this present generation is taking, I wonder if we've been aiming at this goal. With all the help we've been given, especially as Christians, are we effective at producing the kinds of kids who are anxious to be used of God to reform the world around them? Are we, as an entire group, known for sending out children from our homes who are not easily snookered by the corrupted world around them? It doesn't appear that we are.

SO LITTLE DIFFERENCE

You'd think with all the resources that have been developed over the past forty years, we'd have a little more to show for ourselves. If we looked at where the Christian movement is on a grand scale, it demonstrates that we've clearly left something out of the equation. The Christian community in the United States numbers in the multi millions. Because such a significant percentage of our country's population claim to be Christians, we are often referred to as a "Christian nation." We've dedicated billions of dollars to our spiritual experience. We have more brick-and-mortar commitments as well as professionally paid personnel dedicated to the development of our Christian walk than any other nation in the world.

Our churches are often extensions of our families' social needs to the point that many serve as evangelical country clubs. We've created a universe parallel to the corrupted world system that provides us with all the amenities we want. We have our own Christian bookstores. They not only provide us with the tools we need for studying the Bible and growing to be more like Christ, but they also provide us with just about any other type of reading we might like. We might have Christian fiction, science fiction, and romance novels. We have Christian radio programs and cable television dedicated to Christian programming around the clock. We have Christian concerts, Christian cruises, Christian vacation resorts. We have our own school systems. We have our own clothing lines. We have our own breath mints.

With all of these assets dedicated to effective Christian living, why are they making so little impact? You can track the rise of the Christian community into a "market group" from the early 1960s.[2] What's ironic is that the "secularization" of the non-Christian community has risen proportionately with our withdrawal from it. The more options the Christian community created for itself, the more our general culture moved toward secular thinking, the corollary being that the less we need to engage the lost world around us, the more it will be left to its own devices.

> What's ironic is that the "secularization" of the non-Christian community has risen proportionately with our withdrawal from it.

But it isn't supposed to be this way. God left our families in communities to serve as porch lights, if you will, for the lost people around us. We are to be the steady glow that helps them find their way out of the darkness. When families are committed to being this light, they are inclined to live more intimately with Christ. They pray more, they study their Bibles more, they care for one another more, they reach out to their neighbors more. Somewhere in all the talk about raising kids, we moved away from this as a priority in our parenting.

The negative effect of creating this Christian parallel universe has been enormous when it comes to raising strong Christian kids. One of the primary roles that God gave Christian parents is to create adults who reflect His heart. A family is, without doubt, the most effective and efficient vehicle to produce the kind of people who can move confidently into the adult world and have a redemptive impact on their culture—that's what we are supposed to be doing.

So why aren't we?

Why is the world we're living in getting more and more secular? Why have we gotten to the point that our culture has become extremely antagonistic toward us living out our faith in the public arena? Why has our culture turned more hedonistic? There are many explanations that people offer as answers to these questions. The standard one is to blame it on Satan, but that doesn't add up. He hasn't been sleepwalking for the past two thousand years and suddenly just awakened. There was something holding him back. There was one fortress that he had a difficult time penetrating: a good, solid family. Parents armed with little more than a vibrant relationship with God consistently served as the ideal springboard for great people. So something changed. We got *scared*. And I think that fear is what motivates so much of the Christian parenting advice we get.

OUR MAPS ARE WRONG

If you're running through territory you've never traveled before, you're only as good as the maps you're depending on. There have been some tragic results in history of people relying on inadequate or inaccurate maps. When I look at the way some Christian parents bring up their children, and the way some Christian "experts" advise them, it's no wonder we seem to have lost our way.

Let me use some broad brushstrokes to categorize a few of the typical parenting methods I see in the Christian community—methods that have led us astray. The first one on my list is the most pervasive model that I see:

1. Fear-Based Parenting.

We're scared of Hollywood, the Internet, the public school system, Halloween, the gay community, drugs, alcohol, rock 'n' roll, rap, partying neighbors, unbelieving softball teams, liberals, and Santa Claus. Our fears *determine* our strategy for parenting. I see it everywhere I go. I hear it echo in the back of a parent's concerns. The moms or dads begin their statement or question to me with the words "I'm afraid of . . ." When I look at how the standard evangelical family has formatted their strategy for parenting, most often I see fear behind the steering wheel.

If you took all the categories of advice that Jesus gave us in the Gospels, you'd find that the longest list is made up of verses where He says, "Don't be afraid." If we have put our faith in Him, we should be the last people to be afraid of just about *anything*! Fear-based parenting is the surest way to create intim-

> Fear-based parenting is the surest way to create intimidated kids.

idated kids. It's also the surest way to raise Christian kids who either don't have any passion for lost people, are indifferent to the things of God, or out-and-out rebel against their parents, their church, and the Lord.

2. Evangelical Behavior-Modification Parenting

This is an offshoot of fear-based parenting that assumes the proper environment, the proper information, the proper education, and the absence of negative influences will increase the chances of a child's turning out well. This parenting plan works from two flawed assumptions: (1) that the battle is primarily outside the child (it's not); and (2) that the spiritual life can be transferred onto a child's heart much like information placed on a computer hard drive (it can't).

The behavior modeled by these families paints a beautiful picture of an ideal Christian family, but it is only one-dimensional. There is very little below the surface that draws on the faith needed to sustain the harsh "hits" from culture or to go into a deep, mature relationship with

God. These are homes where God rules in the head but seldom gets to move in the heart.

3. Image-Control Parenting

This is a checklist method of parenting that is part of the seduction of legalism. My parents employed this kind of parenting model in the early years of raising their kids. Image-control parenting assumes that people will know you are a good Christian parent raising nice Christian offspring by your church attendance, the way you dress (or don't dress), the way you cut your hair (or don't), the words and expressions you use (or don't use), the schools you attend (or don't attend), the movies you see (or don't see), the amount of Scripture you can quote, the version of the Bible you read, and the kinds of treats you give out for Halloween (if you participate at all).

The problem with this form of parenting is not in the things these parents either do or don't do. For the most part, these are well-meaning people trying to make good choices, but they make them for the *wrong reasons*! Doing good things for wrong reasons consistently brings unfavorable results. Unfortunately, kids can tell when we are living by a checklist rather than trusting in God to lead us.

4. High-Control Parenting

There is a vast difference between parents who keep their children *under* control and parents who control *them*. High-control parenting happens when we leverage the strength of our personality or our position against our children's weaknesses to get them to meet our *selfish* agenda. This form of parenting is fueled by a combination of toxic fear, toxic anger, toxic bondage, toxic shame, and toxic strength. What's sad is how prevalent this form of parenting is in Christian homes.

What makes it so difficult to address is the fact that the last people to see themselves as parenting this way are the very parents who are most guilty of using it as their primary mode of overseeing their kids. High-control parents are blind to how they are treating their children because high-controllers can always morally justify every move they make. Because they are so convinced that their controlling tendency is *right*, they can't see how destructive its effect is on their children.

High-control parenting brings out the worst in children. So high-control parents ultimately get frustrated with the results of their parenting efforts but are usually the last to figure out that they were primarily at fault. (I wrote an entire book addressing this high-control problem in families titled *How to Deal With Powerful Personalities*.[3])

> High-control parenting happens when we leverage the strength of our personality against our children's weaknesses to get them to meet our selfish agenda.

5. Herd-Mentality Parenting

These are parents who follow the crowd. If the crowd is overscheduling their kids with sports, extracurricular activities, and every event the church has to offer, they do, too. These parents aren't known for thinking as individuals. Instead they follow the fads in how they eat, dress, vacation, educate their kids, play, and worship. Rather than pray for guidance and study each of their children to determine what is best for that child, they look around and parent like everyone else is doing.

6. Duct-Tape Parenting

Rather than figure out how to fix their parenting issues, these families cope by patching their problems. Temporary solutions are sought when crises arise. These families are usually running on empty—too busy, too many bills, and too focused on the immediate rather than the permanent.

7. Life-Support or 911 Parenting

These homes are much like the duct-tape families but with the added feature that a particular crisis is dominating their focus. They may be consumed with a medical or economic crisis. Or the crisis may be the result of the deterioration or collapse of a marriage. Sometimes these parents have had a shortchanged childhood or other painful past and have serious wounds to their hearts.

Fear actually runs through all these methods of parenting. Some of these methods can fake moms or dads into thinking that they're on target, but the proof is in the product. For the most part, these methods are no fun for parents and steal a lot of joy from the kids. We all recognize that there are some things about parenting that will never be fun and aren't supposed to be. For the most part, however, a home should be a place that brings the best out in everyone and grooms children for confident and effective adulthood.

HOW WE VIEW GOD DETERMINES HOW WE PARENT OUR CHILDREN

All the parenting styles listed above have this in common: They are the result of a parent's theology. Their theology is a combination of the way they view God and the way they think He views them. If we have flawed theology regarding God's attitude toward us, it can automatically create a chain reaction of flawed decisions in how we raise our children. It can also set up our children to miss the joy of God, the heart of God, and the power of God in their personal lives. This is a recipe for the child to rebel and reject a parent's primary belief system.

Two overarching attitudes mark these defective parenting styles, and both are the result of missing the major message of God's grace that permeates Scripture. Let me frame these two attitudes before I offer a much better alternative. A clear understanding of these two defective attitudes—which I call **judgmental parents** and **legalistic parents**—will also help you as we reference them throughout the rest of the book. Let's look at the characteristics of each before I offer you a radical alternative.

Judgmental parents spend most of their time making sure their family is better than the ones around them. They live to monitor everyone else. Their children are supposed to support their concerns about what is wrong with everyone around them. If you were watching them in action, you would notice them pointing their fingers at others and having little to do with anyone who doesn't see life their way. They can be especially hard on children who don't accept their narrow view of life.

Their advice to their children would be a mixture of:

→ "God is watching you, and so am I."

→ "You may be bad, but you're better than so-and-so."

When it comes to boundaries, their exhortation to their children would be: "If it feels good, it's probably wrong!" When it comes to God, they are so distracted by looking down on other families that don't see life their way, they don't really enjoy God much. God has something to say about them: "If you think you can judge others, you are wrong. When you judge them, you are really judging yourself guilty, because you do the same things they do" (Romans 2:1 NCV).

Legalistic parents spend most of their time trying to make sure their family does everything right. They live to keep score of their good deeds. Their children are supposed to help them stack up "brownie points" with God. If you watch them in action, they appear burdened and stressed out. They are especially hard on children who don't toe the line. Their advice to their children would be a mixture of:

→ "You owe God, so you better get busy."

→ "You may be bad, but if you try harder, you can ultimately please God."

When it comes to boundaries, their exhortation to their children would be: "If it feels good, stop it!" They assume that what God *demands* of them should be their primary business. When it comes to

God, they feel they need to reimburse Him, but God has something to say to them: "People cannot do any work that will make them right with God" (Romans 4:5 NCV).[4]

Do you see that streak of fear running through each of these? It's pervasive—and toxic. It's the surest way to make your children miserable throughout their childhood and ensure them of a fairly hopeless future. (I should note that it is possible to have these two different parenting styles playing out between the mother and the father.)

I feel confident that were we to pin down any of these parents and quiz them about their children, we would come away convinced that they dearly love their kids and want the best for them. Their children may leave these homes feeling loved, but they will also feel something else. Kids with **judgmental parents** tend to leave home with a feeling of spiritual elitism. Kids with **legalistic parents** leave home feeling guilty. They often want nothing to do with the method their parents used to raise them, and they usually live their lives in stark contrast to the values they were raised with.

What can we do? What is the alternative? How can we spare our children and ourselves the heartache that comes with raising our children by such destructive methods?

We start by surrendering our fears to the God who loves us and has a fabulous plan for our family. We are much like the exiles of Israel surrounded by a completely hostile world. God's message to them in that desperate situation could be summed up in three words: "Don't be afraid." Listen to what God said to them through the prophet Jeremiah:

> "For I know the plans I have for you," declares the LORD, "plans to prosper you and not to harm you, plans to give you hope and a future." (Jeremiah 29:11)

a Radical way to Parent

I've got good news! I found the cover of the puzzle box. It shows exactly what our kids are supposed to look like when they finally head out on their own. I found the box cover in the Bible, of all places, and it's something my wife and I have been using to raise our own children for the past few decades. We've been extremely pleased with the results. We've even used the box cover as the template for our marriage, and what's even more amazing is that it's even spilled over into our relationships with our friends as well as strangers. This new model for parenting can be summarized in one word: grace! It's actually not new; it just hasn't gotten much attention among the Christian parenting community.

What does a grace-based family look like?

Grace-based parents spend their time entrusting themselves to Christ. They live to know God more. Their children are the daily recipients of the grace these parents are enjoying from the Lord. If you watch them in action, they appear to be peaceful and very much in love with God. They are especially graceful when their children are hardest to love. Their advice to their children would be a mixture of:

➔ "You are a gift from God; go make a difference."

➔ "You may struggle doing the right thing sometimes, but you're forgiven."

When it comes to boundaries, their exhortation to their children would be: "If it feels good, examine it." When it comes to God, they feel they need to seek Him more every day. Most of the time, they're just *grateful* people. God has something to say to them: "Those who are right with God will live by trusting in him" (Romans 1:17 NCV).[5]

> Grace-based families are a breath of fresh air.

Grace-based families are a breath of fresh air. They process their day-to-day life with an air of confidence that comes from knowing God profoundly loves them. The key characteristic of grace-based families is that they aren't afraid. They are especially unafraid of all the evil around them. They take their cues straight from King David's playbook:

> Even though I walk through the valley of the shadow of death, *I will fear no evil, for you are with me;* your rod and your staff, they comfort me. (Psalm 23:4, emphasis mine)

This changes the way children view their parents and the choices they make on their behalf. It also gives children a much more attractive view of their parents' faith. Parents who operate by grace instead of by a checklist or popular opinion are a lot easier for their children to trust. And when a child's world is falling apart, he is more inclined to turn to parents whose primary description is "grace."

Grace-based parents have a keen awareness of their feet of clay. They understand their own propensity toward sin. This makes the grace and forgiveness they received from Christ much more appreciated. It stirs them to love and good deeds *for the right reasons*. They aren't driven by guilt and a need to do penance. The last thing they want to do is stand in judgment of struggling people. They see themselves in these people and understand just how much of God's love they have received. They are more inclined to want to love these people and care for the genuine needs in their life.

This sounds a lot like how Jesus lived His life. He, who knew no sin, became sin for us, that in Him we might become the righteousness of God.[6]

GOD'S PATH OF GRACE

I'm urging you to raise your children the way God raises His. The primary word that defines how God deals with His children is *grace*. Grace does not exclude obedience, respect, boundaries, or discipline, but it does determine the climate in which these important parts of parenting are carried out. You may be weird and quirky, but God loves you through His grace with all of your weirdness and quirkiness. You may feel extremely inadequate and fragile in key areas of your life, but God comes alongside you in those very areas of weakness and carries you through with His grace.[7] You may be frustrated, hurt, and even angry with God, but His grace allows you to candidly, confidently, and boldly approach His "throne of grace."[8] His grace is there for you when you fail, when you fall, and when you make huge mistakes.

This kind of grace makes all the difference in the world when it's coming from God, through you, to your children. Children brought up in homes where they are free to be different, vulnerable, candid, and to make mistakes learn firsthand what the genuine love of God looks like.

Grace frees you to take your cues from God on all the big decisions you face in raising your kids. One of the characteristics of God's grace is how much latitude He grants within His clear moral boundaries to make choices. Grace allows you to tailor your parenting style and decisions to the unique bent of your child.[9] God is a God of variety, and He deals with us accordingly.

Take zebras. God hasn't painted the same stripes on any of them. Every person's fingerprints are original. He hasn't let two snowflakes drop from the sky that were identical. He hasn't painted any two sunsets the same. He's an original God who wants to have an original relationship with you and your children.

SHOWING A LITTLE LATITUDE

God will even let you tailor your discipline style to one that works best with your child, with your personal history, and with what the context calls for. When it comes to evangelizing your children, once again His grace is amazing. You can actually wait on God to move in your children's lives and not let your fears incline you to jump the gun or give Him a little help. When it comes to educating your children, His grace can lead you to many options—all of them excellent—because you are being led by your confidence in Him rather than your fears of your culture.

Speaking of fears, if your child attends the public school system, a grace-based family makes it easier for him or her to succeed because you aren't intimidated by the inherent shortcomings inside the public school system. And if you aren't afraid of what's out there, it's a lot easier for your children to thrive spiritually inside the antagonistic environment they might encounter at school.

BOUNDARIES

The *truth* that is an inseparable part of *grace* will help you determine where to set the boundaries in their lives. God's moral law is non-negotiable, but how you apply it in things like entertainment, dating, clothing, styles, and fads is easier when you're responding from a passionate relationship with Christ rather than some checklist made up by someone who's never met you or your children. Decisions are passed through the filter of God's grace. God helps grace-based parents see what matters and what doesn't matter; what is an issue and what isn't an issue.

> God helps grace-based parents see what matters and what doesn't matter.

His grace helps you see whether to write the rules in pencil or in blood. Your children will be the daily recipients of the number one characteristic of God that has drawn people to Him since the Creation.

IT'S AN ADVENTURE

I want to show you a whole new way of looking at your role as a parent. It's also a great way to bring out the best in those grandchildren you may have pictures of on your refrigerator. This adventure is going to be divided into two parts. The first part of our adventure will focus on the *goal* of our parenting efforts, and the second part will focus on the *delivery system* of those efforts. Both of them launch from grace.

22

I want to introduce the goal of grace-based parenting by first giving you a little quiz . . .

THE GOAL . . . AND THE QUIZ

I'm going to ask you a simple question that will determine if you are even in the right area code when it comes to raising great kids.

"What are the fundamental, driving inner needs that your child was born with?"

Your ability to answer this question *precisely* is key to your being able to effectively groom your children for the future. If you are struggling with the answer, however, don't feel badly. Most parents can't list all three needs correctly.

Most parents would get one of the needs (love) right, but they would be hard-pressed to define what that need looks like once it's fully met. The rest would offer answers like food, clothing, shelter (physical needs, but not driving inner needs), education (an intellectual need, but not one of the driving inner needs), or salvation (another good guess, but not one of the driving inner needs of a child). Regarding salvation, people aren't necessarily born *feeling* that they *need* a Savior, and some people die unconvinced that they ever did.

These driving inner needs are the ones that Adam and Eve were *created* with. They had them *before* what is traditionally known as "the Fall"—*before* they needed to be redeemed. These needs were the logical conclusion of being made in God's image. That's why, when these needs are properly met, they are ultimately met in Him. Therefore, it is essential that these needs be the focal point of a wise parent's efforts.

Which takes us back to our quiz. If you're tracking with me, I've said that all children are born with three driving inner needs, but few parents could tell you what they are. Here's what's interesting: There is *one person* who, if you handed him a piece of paper and a pen, would be able to write out the answers to the three driving inner needs perfectly. His name is . . .

Satan.

He knows *exactly* what drives our children, and he is working even as you are reading this book to meet your child's three driving inner needs in counterfeit ways. He went after these needs when he tempted Eve in the Garden of Eden (Genesis 3:1–6). He knew these needs were the basic components of the divine DNA since we were created in God's image. That's why he appealed to these needs. He even appealed to them when he tried but failed to tempt Jesus in the wilderness (Matthew 4:1–11). Every time you see him making a move on your children, he's offering them a knockoff solution to one or a combination of these three inner needs.

If we aren't processing everything we say or do through the filter of these three inner needs, we're going to have a difficult time upstaging the counterfeits that Satan offers so effectively to our children. Raising your children in a spiritual cocoon won't help because Satan operates *inside* it. He appeals to your child's heart. Plus, he isn't our only competition. The world system and our children's inner bent toward selfishness can also do a pretty good number on our efforts.

We need more than knowledge of these three inner needs. We need a plan to let God help us meet these needs properly in our children so that when they finally leave our sphere of influence as adults, these "needs" are actually transformed into "assets"—part of their emotional and spiritual DNA as well.

Grace-based parents keep these three driving inner needs of their children in the *foreground* of their day-to-day involvement with them, and everything else drops to the background. And I mean *everything*. You may be doing a lot of things each day that make up your role as a parent: taking them to school or homeschooling them; sitting at a soccer game; taking them to the library; or giving them the third degree about what time they got in last night. But when you're committed to grace-based parenting, all these actions are processed through the filter of meeting your child's driving inner needs.

So, without further fanfare, your child's three driving inner needs are

1. A need for security

2. A need for significance

3. A need for strength

In this book, we'll learn that the way to meet these needs is by giving your children three valuable gifts: **love, purpose,** and **hope.** If we've done our job adequately, our children should leave our homes with a love that is secure, a purpose that is significant, and a hope that is strong.

THE DELIVERY SYSTEM

The second part of developing a grace-based style of parenting has to do with the way you meet these three inner needs on a day-to-day basis. There is an environment or *ambiance* that children can grow up in that enables these three driving inner needs to turn into adult assets. It's an environment that oozes grace. Grace-based parenting is the antithesis of every parenting model listed earlier in this chapter—especially the fear-based and the high-control parenting.

Grace is not so much what we do as parents, but *how* we do what we do. Grace is the best advertisement for a personal relationship with the living God. As I stated earlier, *it's the way He parents us.* It is also the best vehicle for parents to find their love, purpose, and hope in Him. We'll learn four characteristics of a grace-based family that consistently enhance our ability to connect with our children's hearts.

Their needs will not be met as a result of your reading this book. Meeting these needs will be the result of your putting what you learned into practice in your life *first.* Why is that? You have the same driving inner needs as they do. You need to know that you are loved, that you have a purpose, and that you have hope. You want to know that you are secure, significant, and strong. It will take time. This is a process, not an event, as the Scripture says, "but grow in the grace and knowledge of our Lord and Savior Jesus Christ" (2 Peter 3:18). As your children see you meeting your need for love, purpose, and hope through your abiding relationship with Christ, your example will put power and authenticity behind your words. Reading this book is the first step in the process. Before you get to the end, you might find there's even more in it for you than there is for your kids.

Meeting the needs that God hard-wired into them at birth and treating them the way God treats us—these are the things that maybe we've missed in our parenting process up until now. And when you specifically place these three inner needs in the forefront of your plan for parenting, they serve as great filters for all the information and advice floating around regarding how to raise your kids.

Here's something else you should know—you'll set your family free.

CHAPTER 2

The Truth
Behind Grace

The scene was a luncheon at a local restaurant, where I was sitting at a table of distinguished World War II veterans. Each had been highly decorated for his courage in the line of duty. One had personally received the Congressional Medal of Honor from President Franklin D. Roosevelt in a White House ceremony.

The battlefield had welded these men's hearts together. I could sense the fraternity between them—a fraternity I could only observe but never join. In addition to their heroic valor on the battlefield, each man had come home from the war and distinguished himself in the world of commerce. Not only was I surrounded by some of the bravest men of the "Greatest Generation," as Tom Brokaw called them, but I was also dining with men who played a huge role in our postwar prosperity.

The luncheon topic that day had to do with exports. The question was simple: What do you think is America's most strategic export? One suggested our banking system; another talked about the hardware and software produced in Silicon Valley and elsewhere in the country. But it was the Medal of Honor recipient who carried the debate. He summarized our greatest American export in one word—freedom. "Products and systems come and go," he said. "The greatest commodity we have to offer the world is freedom."

A similar luncheon was held a half century ago in England. The people around the table were not held together by the bonds of physical war but by the bonds of spiritual war. The general topic was comparative religions, which sparked a debate on the question of Christianity's most valuable distinction. What separated Christianity from every other religion in the world?

One suggested the Incarnation, another the resurrection of Christ. It was pointed out, however, that these two vital features of Christianity were also part of the deities of other religions. C. S. Lewis, who joined the debate late, uttered the answer as soon as he heard the topic of the day. "Oh, that's easy," said perhaps the greatest Christian apologist of the twentieth century. "It's grace."[1]

BOTTOM LINE

The learned British author was right. The most distinguishing part of the Christian faith is grace—that wonderful gift offered by God to undeserving people like you and me that makes us fall in love with the Savior. Grace is what attracts us to Him and what confirms His love for us over and over. God's grace has the power to transform the most hardened, indifferent soul into a person spilling over with kindness. If God our heavenly Father is the perfect Father, and the primary way that He deals with us as humans is through the power of His grace, it stands to reason that grace forms the best template for bringing out the best in our own children.

One reason that C. S. Lewis was revered as a great thinker was his ability to quickly determine the bottom line. There comes a point in making a major purchase or moving forward in an important relationship when we all ask the same question: What's the bottom line?

How much is this going to cost me? Do I have a chance with you?

If something as significant as Christianity has a bottom line, then it makes sense that there should be a bottom line to our role as parents. When all is said and done, we want to know what we are supposed to be accomplishing. Once we know that answer, it should affect every interaction with our children.

> If something as significant as Christianity has a bottom line, then it makes sense that there should be a bottom line to our role as parents.

For instance, if you believe that our country's best export is freedom, then that colors how you conduct foreign policy, do international business, handle immigration, and even fight wars. In the same way, if the bottom line of parenting is grace, then that should affect how you develop goals for your children, how you handle discipline, how you process their fears, how you deal with their quirks and idiosyncrasies, and how you respond to their fads. Grace keeps you from clamping down on their spirits when they move through awkward transitions and walk through the valley of the shadow of adolescence. The reason grace makes the most sense as a bottom line for parenting is because of grace's *eternal* appeal to the human heart.

There's an interesting tie-in between grace's work in a human heart and the sense of freedom that person enjoys in life. In the process of making grace the template for your role as a parent, you get to export true freedom to your child's inner core.

QUESTIONING THE PREMISE

Perhaps you feel more comfortable saying that the bottom line of Christianity is Christ. After all, it says of Him in Scripture that:

> He is the image of the invisible God, the firstborn over all creation.
> For by him all things were created: things in heaven and on earth,

visible and invisible, whether thrones or powers or rulers or authorities; all things were created by him and for him. He is before all things, and in him all things hold together. (Colossians 1:15–17)

I don't question for a second that the core of Christianity is Jesus. Sooner or later, our children must ultimately have an encounter with God through His Son, Jesus. But what is it about Jesus that inclines us to cast our lot with a simple carpenter from an obscure, ancient village? It's because of His grace—grace He has shown us by first purchasing us from the depths of our lost condition. It's His grace that loves us when we're being foolish, or stubborn, or selfish, or mean-spirited.

Grace sounds like a great tool to have in a parent's toolbox. It's hard bringing out the best in children when they seem committed to bringing out the worst in us. We need something that can slip through the creases of their tough facades. God's grace has a way of melting itself into the hardest of hearts.

Grace can also help you know what matters and what doesn't. It helps you give kids a lot of freedom to simply be "kids" and keeps you from living in a reactive mode as they go through certain stages. Without grace, you can turn high standards and strong moral convictions into knives that cut deeply into the inner recesses of your children's hearts.

WHEN OUR STANDARDS TURN TOXIC

One Sunday morning, I stood in the back of the gymnasium that is the staging area for our church's high-school ministry. The gym was packed with several hundred students singing worship songs. The music was definitely not "unplugged." There was a loud synthesizer, electric guitars, a thumping bass, and a drummer driving the beat. A father named Tom—a casual acquaintance—sidled up next to me. I knew he placed very high standards on his children, enforced his standards with strict discipline, and was quite distraught over the direction the youth culture was taking. He was standing in the back of the gym, trying to determine whether to let his high-school-age children join the youth group.

Tom didn't like much of what he saw or heard. When he noticed me, his attitude took a turn for the worse.

"I can't believe you allow your kids to be exposed to this garbage!" he hissed. He knew I wrote books about parenting, and from my children's presence in this youth group, he assumed I felt comfortable with what I was seeing. He was correct.

"What's wrong?" I asked.

"The music, for openers," he said. I could tell that Tom was one of those who believed that our culture was in moral decline and that the church had co-opted the trappings of a corrupted world system. For him, if it had a beat, then it had to be bad.

I will concede that there's ample evidence to support the different points of his position. I don't want to trivialize any of our real problems, but we must keep in mind that these types of concerns have *always* existed in our nation's history. They've also existed in all free societies over the past two millenniums.

Tom felt that the style of music, the way the kids were allowed to dress, and the way the leadership communicated their message was a sellout.

I pointed out that the kids in the group covered the spectrum. I saw conservatively dressed kids and kids that looked like they'd stepped out of an Abercrombie & Fitch catalog. I noticed a generous number of pierced bellybuttons, some tattoos, and a lot of midriffs showing. Many of the teens tinted their hair or wore it in different styles.

Tom, like many people, assumed that these things were indications of some huge problem brewing inside. Not necessarily. I was aware of kids in the group who were struggling with drugs, premarital sex, and with serious rebellion. But you couldn't tell who they were by *looking* at them. More important, they were there in church—the hospital that God left behind for them. They were the very kinds of kids I *wanted* to see in our youth group, rubbing shoulders with young people serious about their faith. Youth ministries reach out and minister to all kinds of young people at various points on their spiritual journey. I felt that these were exactly the kind of young people I wanted my kids to reach out to. But Tom was one of those types of parents who wanted to raise "safe" kids. My wife and I would rather raise *strong* kids, and a grace-based environment makes that easier to accomplish.

> My wife and I would rather raise strong kids, and a grace-based environment makes that easier to accomplish.

I invited Tom to step into a nearby kitchen so that his seething wouldn't disturb the gathering. From our vantage point, we could continue observing the crowd without them hearing what we were saying.

"Look at these kids!" he exclaimed. "The girls look like they just came from orientation at Hooters. Some of these guys look like they'd strip your car during Communion."

What I saw was a group of kids that represented the social, intellectual, and spiritual strata found in Christian homes. "Tom," I said, "how can you draw such ridiculous assumptions simply because these kids' outfits don't meet your approval? You don't know any of them."

"I know enough that this is no place to be sending my kids to youth group. It's not just their outfits, Tim, it's their overall attitude." Somehow he felt that by looking at a couple hundred kids with their backs to us he could evaluate the spirits within their hearts. "Look at those worship leaders. They're acting like they're MCs on some MTV video countdown."

"Tom, these kids are worshiping the Lord. Listen to the words they're singing. Those lyrics are straight from Scripture."

He wasn't paying any attention to me. He was just getting madder by the minute. Then he spied a half-dozen boys in the very last row. "I can't stand it! It's so disrespectful!" he complained.

"What do you mean, Tom?" I thought that he had observed one

of them opening up a *Penthouse* magazine instead of his Bible. Whatever it was, it sure was bothering Tom.

"It's these guys right here in front of us. They're wearing their hats right here in church, and they've got them on *backward*. Someone should do something. Heck, I'll do it myself."

"Do what?" I started to block his exit from the kitchen.

"I'm going to rip those hats right off their disrespectful heads."

For the first time in my life, I was watching a Pharisee flip out. Here was a man who evaluated sincerity and spiritual maturity by external standards that meant *nothing*. If he had his way, he'd clean house in the youth department at our church and replace the leadership with people who agreed with his strict and narrow view of acceptability.

Having been a youth pastor for many years, I figured out early on that reaching young people is a lot like fishing. When it comes to luring fish, it's best to put on the hook something they like to eat, not what you like. Tom was elevating his personal taste to a level of biblical authority, and he was about to humiliate some nice kids who were minding their own business and trying to worship God.

"You're not going to do any such thing, Tom. Just leave them alone; they aren't doing anything disrespectful to God." I knew one of those boys. His father had died when he was ten years old. He was trying hard to find answers to some of the missing pieces in his life. There was no way I was going to let this passionate but misguided father do anything to any of those boys. The thought came to me that as these high-school students were standing out in the gymnasium worshiping, two fathers were in the kitchen having a verbal face-off with clenched fists at their sides.

ONLY SEEING HALF THE PICTURE

No punches were exchanged, no blood ended up on the church's kitchen floor, but a lengthy conversation followed outside in a sitting area. In the process of the conversation, I asked Tom what had happened to his sense of grace. That's when he blurted out one of the standard rebukes to people who preach grace. "Tim, you know full well that grace is just a smoke screen for license. Parents preoccupied with grace are just pushovers who don't want to teach their kids to obey what God commands."

Grace certainly has its share of enemies. There are those enemies who want to camp on the truth of the Bible and say that life is black and white with little nuance. Parents like Tom assume that to show grace is to go soft on moral standards. They get a lot of fuel for this skewed opinion of grace from the parents who use grace as their excuse for not enforcing rules. A family without clearly defined rules and standards could never be a grace-based family. It's too busy being a nightmare to live in.

Tom was also making a mistake that many people wrapped up in legalistic parenting make. They look on grace as a cop-out—something used by parents who don't want to take any of the unpopular stands that often accompany moral convictions. Those who reject a grace-based environment often lament our decline into secularism. They decry the absence of standards. They think grace allows children to do their own thing and make their own decisions at the expense of moral absolutes. They believe grace is light on discipline and doesn't enforce rules.

None of these views have anything to do with what real biblical grace is about, as we'll soon see.

THE INSEPARABLE NATURE OF GRACE AND TRUTH

We can see God's heart in the description of Jesus that the apostle John gave in his opening remarks to his gospel.

> In the beginning was the Word, and the Word was with God, and the Word was God . . . The Word became flesh and made his dwelling among us. We have seen his glory, the glory of the One and Only, who came from the Father, *full of grace and truth*. (John 1:1, 14, emphasis mine)

Notice that there isn't a comma between grace and truth in the description of Christ. John isn't handing us a laundry list of Messiah's character traits. He is saying that Christ is filled with grace *and* truth, not grace *or* truth, or *some* grace and *some* truth. He is describing two parts that make up a single whole.

That reminds me of the time I read about a set of Siamese twins who could not be separated because they shared the same heart and respiratory system. The way their organs were arranged inside them, doctors didn't even have an option to separate them and allow one to live and the other to die. For them, to eliminate either was to kill them both.

So it is with the issue of grace. You can't have grace when you have rules but little relationship. In fact, that is the ideal formula for raising rebellious kids. You cannot assume that you are even in the area code of grace if your way of raising kids is confined to making sure they adhere to a clear set of guidelines. Guys like Tom are blind to this because they have such a strong passion for godly obedience. If any of their children balk at their unreasonableness, they can always drop the Ephesians 6:1 grenade on them. That's the passage where Paul admonished children to obey their parents in the Lord, for it is the right thing to do.

Parents like Tom can easily open a Bible and show you chapter and verse to defend their thinking. Since they can use the Bible to defend their strict views on hairstyles, clothing styles, and music styles, it makes it hard to argue with them. They can even justify why they would keep their children away from any other kids and influences that don't meet their strict code. They slip over a thin line, however. Many times they have imposed their personal taste into the argument and are misusing the Bible to support it.

For instance, God gave us Ephesians 6:1 to help children respond to their parents' leadership and authority. He didn't mean for parents to use it to pistol-whip their kids. One of the standard ploys of grace-less Christian parents is to abuse Scripture to get their own way. I've seen husbands do the same thing with a verse that God directed to their wives earlier in Ephesians. In these verses, God presents guidelines for how married people should respond to each other and how parents and children should interact.

Ephesians 5:22 says, "Wives, submit to your husbands as to the Lord." This verse is not directed to husbands. It starts out, "Wives . . ." But that doesn't stop a lot of men from using this verse like some kind of ball-peen hammer to metaphorically whack their wives into submission to their selfish agenda. Ephesians 5:22 is between a wife and God, not a husband and a wife. God speaks directly to husbands a few verses later (verse 25) when He says, "Husbands, love your wives, just as Christ loved the church." Likewise, women aren't supposed to use this verse to remind their husbands of how short of the mark they fall. These verses aren't weapons, and to use them as such misses the point of God's grace.

If fathers like Tom really want a verse regarding their relationship with their children, it can be found just a few sentences after Ephesians 6:1. In 6:4 it says, "Fathers, do not exasperate your children; instead, bring them up in the training and instruction of the Lord." The Greek word translated "exasperate" means literally to *irritate beyond measure*.[2] Parents like Tom can be guilty of irritating their children beyond measure by turning *personal* issues into *spiritual* issues. This can undermine the genuine things he and his wife might be doing to "bring them up in the training and instruction of the Lord." (This is where we need to have a theology check: Notice that Ephesians 6:4 says to bring children up in "the training and instruction of the *Lord*," who is also known as Jesus, who was "filled with *grace* and *truth*.")

The apostle Paul admonishes fathers again in Colossians 3:21 when he writes, "Fathers, do not embitter your children, or they will become discouraged." The word translated "embitter" literally means to *rouse them to strife*.[3] What Paul is talking about is unnecessarily ticking off children. It's doing things that cause them to resent you. Think about it: What has Christ done to provoke you or "irritate you beyond measure"? Name an action of God's that has roused you to strife or caused you to resent Him. That's not the way God operates. He's a graceful Father who cherishes His children and treats them in a way that draws them to His heart and the safety and security of His everlasting arms.

THE OTHER EXTREME

Rules not tempered by grace block relationships with our children and lead to rebellion. On the other side, relationships without rules don't result in grace either. In fact, that is the ideal formula for raising resentful kids. Which brings up a couple I met named Dave and Connie. I was speaking at their church one Sunday, and my message that morning was the same topic as this book—"Grace-Based Families." Following my speaking at two worship services, Dave and Connie were supposed to take care of me for lunch and then drop me off back at my hotel room. Rather than drive me to a restaurant, they thought I might enjoy the relaxing atmosphere of their home. Dave said Connie was a terrific cook, and they figured it would give me a chance to meet their kids. That sounded like a great idea to me. Besides, I get tired of restaurant food.

> Rules not tempered by grace block relationships with our children and lead to rebellion. On the other side, relationships without rules don't result in grace either.

Connie's reputation as a cook was well founded, and I enjoyed meeting their children, ages eighteen, fifteen, and thirteen—boy, girl, boy. A fourth young person, their daughter's boyfriend, joined us. While Connie cooked and Dave helped out, I visited with their children and got to know some things about their interests. It turns out that the eighteen-year-old boy was a musician. We stopped by his room, where he showed me a pile of guitars, amps, and stage paraphernalia. Like most teenagers, posters adorned the walls, including three that looked like they belonged in the swimsuit issue of *Sports Illustrated*.

I didn't get to spend any personal time with the thirteen-year-old boy. I wish that I could have, but I did hear an exchange between him and his older brother. They got involved in some dispute that disintegrated into vicious name-calling and the use of certain words that would automatically qualify a film to be rated R.

After the kids were excused from lunch, I visited with my host and hostess for a while before Dave grabbed his car keys to take me back to my hotel. As we passed through the family room, I glanced at the TV to check out the score of the football game. That's when I noticed Dave and Connie's fifteen-year-old daughter lying on the couch with her boyfriend. They weren't just lying side by side watching the game. They were lying on top of each other having a major make-out session right there in the family room. Dave said nothing and did nothing.

On the trip to my hotel, Dave told me how much he "resonated" with my message about grace-based parenting. "That's what Connie and I have been committed to from the beginning," he said.

Really? I thought, wondering if I should speak up or shut up. After all, I wanted to be a "grace-based" guest. What I had viewed in his house, however, was a family in desperate need of the truth dimension of grace. I figured that staying silent would be anything but graceful. I decided to creep gingerly into a conversation about some of the things I saw that contradicted a "grace and truth" view of grace.

"Dave, you and Connie have taken good care of me today. I'm grateful. And I'm glad you resonated with my message. Grace is vital to strong families and raising kids equipped for the future. Can I ask you a couple of close-to-the-heart questions about how you and Connie view grace?" After I got his permission, I plowed right in and asked him about the racy posters, the name-calling, and the steamy "halftime entertainment" his daughter and boyfriend were enjoying.

David replied that he and Connie had talked to their son about his posters, to the boys about their fighting and name-calling, and to their daughter about the level of intimacy she was having with her boyfriend. But that's as far as it went. They just "talked." They felt that their unconditional love and acceptance would ultimately win out. Dave said he not only wanted to show them grace, but he wanted them to enjoy the grace that God offers to them even though they are making bad choices.

After he made this statement, our conversation was cut short by my arrival at the hotel. He had some things he had to do that afternoon, and so did I. I closed our conversation by mentioning to him the inseparable nature of truth and grace. "It's not just about standing for the truth," I said, "but living for the truth as well. It means that behavior that is clearly unacceptable to God shouldn't be condoned or tolerated. Grace is not to be diminished by taking advantage of it. I believe the apostle Paul was trying to make that point in the first part of Romans 6. You might want to review that passage."

"Thank you," he said. "I should do that." As soon as Dave said that, I could tell he didn't really *hear* what I was saying. That's too bad because a grace-based home could never condone with silence or inaction the kind of behavior his kids were into.

CHEAP GRACE

What David was doing by allwoing his kids to continue their behavior was to cheapen grace. I have no way of knowing if he read Romans 6, but if David did, he would see why Paul not only tells us that we shouldn't do that, but he also mentions why:

> What shall we say, then? Shall we go on sinning so that grace may increase? By no means! We died to sin; how can we live in it any longer? (Romans 6:1–2)

Paul understood what it meant to struggle to live a holy life. He also knew that in spite of his feet of clay, his love from God was secure. Paul understood the grace of God—that it isn't based on our merits. But even with all of that understood, Paul did not see God's grace as a "Get Out of Responsibility Free" card. He knew that his corrupted fallen nature died with Christ on the cross. To continue to live according to his corrupted fallen nature was to insult Christ's work for him on the cross and to deny His power to give him victory over his sin.

Contrary to what the Toms and the Davids of this world think, grace does not lower the standards in our homes; it raises them. It doesn't push people away from holiness; it pushes them toward it. It doesn't cause them to despise truth; it propels them to embrace truth all the more. It encourages people to aim higher in their relationship with God and helps them dream bigger dreams. Cheap grace, on the other hand, holds people down and sets them up for heartache.

> grace does not lower the standards in our homes; it raises them.

Randy Alcorn says in his book *The Grace and Truth Paradox*, "The Christian life is far more than sin management. Behavior modification that's not empowered by God's heart-changing grace is self-righteous, as repugnant to God as the worst sins people gossip about. Children who grow up with graceless truth are repelled by self-righteousness and attracted to the world's slickly marketed grace-substitutes."[4] Guys like Tom may take pride in how well their children behave, but the harsh way Tom gets his results, and the connection he builds between their behavior and their acceptance by God, sets them up to look elsewhere for their security, significance, and strength. It is the lack of grace in well-behaved homes that turns children's hearts away from God when they're finally too big to intimidate and too old to control.

"I have come to see legalism," says author Philip Yancey, "in its pursuit of false purity as an elaborate scheme of grace avoidance. You can know the law by heart without knowing the heart of it."[5] There is a place for rules, even for strictness, in a grace-based home, but how they are presented makes all the difference on how they are received.

On the other hand, seeing grace as an excuse not to parent your children within the boundaries of godliness is equally repugnant to God. It is not grace that condones the crooked paths our children may take. Rather it is cowardice, laziness, and selfishness. Home has got to be a place where our children are safe from the traps of the world and assured that they have parents who won't surrender God's standards— even to them. Look at what this passage in Titus reveals about grace going hand in hand with godliness.

> For the grace of God that brings salvation has appeared to all men. It teaches us to say "No" to ungodliness and worldly passions, and to live self-controlled, upright and godly lives in this present age, while we wait for the blessed hope—the glorious appearing of our great God and Savior, Jesus Christ, who gave himself for us to redeem us from all wickedness and to purify for himself a people that are his very own, eager to do what is good. (Titus 2:11–14)

KEEPING THE LIGHTS ON

I remember a hike I took once to see an ancient lighthouse on Chesapeake Bay. It was farther than I had been told, and the day was hotter than I had anticipated. But I'm a sucker for lighthouses. I've gone many miles out of my way to see these timeless symbols of grace.

This lighthouse on Chesapeake Bay began shining its bright light just a few decades after we had gained our independence from England. For more than two hundred years, this lighthouse had maintained its clear beam of light as our nation grew into the greatest exporter of freedom in the history of the world.

Lighthouses represent hope to sailors who have lost their way. They are that steady stream of truth that glows through the darkness and marks the safest way through the night. It doesn't matter what season it is for those at sea or what the immediate forecast has churned up. These beacons of grace pierce the darkness and the fog that surrounds them. They bring the sighs of relief from worried captains and cheers from confused sailors manning the sails.

So I was naturally disappointed to make the trek only to discover this lighthouse was now just a "house." The slender tower on the edge of a bluff offered grace to no one, its main light dimmed more than a decade earlier. Maintenance costs were too high, I learned.

As it stood now, this darkened tower symbolized too many parents who are letting their lights dim and their children crash along the rocks. That's a shame because God places parents as a light on a hill for their family. It is our job to send out a clear signal that helps our children get their bearings and keep their wits. We're there to warn them away from rocks and shallow shoals. We're there to guide them safely back into the center of the channel when they've wandered off. We are a *lighthouse*, permanently established to show them the way home. Without us keeping that steady light shining, our children don't stand much of a chance of making it through the turbulent years of childhood without serious consequences.

> We are a lighthouse, permanently established to show them the way home.

As Scripture says:

In the same way, let your light shine before men, that they may see your good deeds and praise your Father in heaven. (Matthew 5:16)

CHAPTER 3

a Secure Love

All children are born with a need to love and be loved, a need to live lives that have meaning, and a need to believe that tomorrow is worth getting up for. Security, significance, and strength—love, purpose, and hope. These are the story lines for great novels and movies, the inspiration for the best songs ever sung. They are three ingredients of a life that finds fulfillment in the God who created these needs. The most effective vehicle God designed to transfer these to a human heart is a grace-based home.

WHAT CAMELOT CAN TEACH US

Perhaps you studied the story in high-school literature class. Maybe you saw the musical or one of the versions that made its way to film—*Camelot*. We're talking about King Arthur. The Knights of the Round Table. This enduring story from British folklore has all the elements of a great epic: An accidental king assumes a throne. He wants to introduce a new ideal to this kingdom he has inherited. He wants to elevate the individual rights and personal values of every member of his kingdom. From the lowest peasant to the highest-pedigreed member of his Round Table—he wants everyone treated as equals. He introduces the rule of law. His knights become the champions of this new order.

And then there's the love triangle that tests all his ideals and convictions. There's Queen Guinevere—his wife, his lover, and his soul mate. She has brought beauty to his throne and joy to his heart. And there's Lancelot, the French knight who has come all the way across the English Channel to join King Arthur's Round Table. He's Arthur's confidant, compatriot, and closest friend.

You know how the story goes. Guinevere loses her heart to Lancelot. The two betray their covenants with King Arthur—she as wife and he as friend. And when they are caught in the compromise, Lancelot escapes to France while Guinevere is brought up on charges. The idealistic young king is placed in checkmate by his own system. On the one hand, there's the rule of law. The queen has cheated on her husband, betrayed her king, and has brought shame to the kingdom. The law dictates that she should die at the stake. Justice must be blind. But in spite of her betrayal, Arthur loves her and is willing to forgive her. And he's willing to forgive Lancelot.

The story of King Arthur and the Knights of the Round Table is a story with grace at its core, a magnificent tale of people not getting what they deserve. But *Camelot* is a flawed story. King Arthur was humiliated and made the butt of jokes throughout his kingdom. The best way for him to redeem his honor as well as maintain the integrity of the Round Table was to permit the courts to carry out the sentence. But his heart ached because of what Guinevere's actions were going to cost her—the flames, the agony, the death. And even though his heart was wrenched by her infidelity, he still longed to show mercy and unconditional love. But he was caught between two conflicting virtues.

You smile when you read about him ordering that the tower lights be lit on the night of her execution. He's anticipating Sir Lancelot coming to her rescue. He wants to make sure Lance and his army can find the castle in the night. You agonize with him as he stares down from his chamber at the executioner, waiting for the signal to light the flames that will immolate his wife. And then just when you think time has run out, Lancelot storms the gate with his soldiers and carries Guinevere away to safety.

In the various book versions I've read and the plays I've seen, this moment is always the same. As he watches from his chamber window and sees his men being overtaken by Lancelot, King Arthur leaps for joy. He *and* the people close to him share his relief. This guilty woman who deserved her fate has been spared.

Camelot really isn't a story of redemption. It's a story of rescue. Of sin unpunished. The guilty slipping away into the night. But *Camelot* is also the story of twisted love and incomplete grace. A king wanted to spare a subject. A husband didn't want to see a cheating wife get her just deserts. Yet the flaw of the story is that justice is circumvented.

The story of King Arthur has similarities to the drama that happened between the King of kings and you and me—His disloyal subjects—but there is a marked contrast. We live our selfish lives and betray our commitment to God as our King. We deserve to pay for our crimes against His holiness. Because of His holiness, He could not permit a rescue to take place that would leave the sin unaccounted for. No tower fires were lit. The guard at the gate was reinforced. Nothing could be allowed to circumvent justice that had to be carried out. Where the stories part is when the King of kings decided to meet the standard of justice and offer us a way of escape. In an act of pure love, the King of kings exchanged places with us and took our punishment with His own life.

> The story of King Arthur has similarities to the drama that happened between the King of kings and you and me—His disloyal subjects—but there is a marked contrast.

At the core of grace is love—a love that delights in us in spite of our sin and comes to us free of charge. Love emanates straight from the heart of God. The Bible uses *love* as both a synonym and an adjective for *God*.

Dear friends, let us love one another, for love comes from God. Everyone who loves has been born of God and knows God. Whoever does not love does not know God, because God is love. This is how God showed his love among us: He sent his one and only Son into the world that we might live through him. This is love: not that we loved God, but that he loved us and sent his Son as an atoning sacrifice for our sins. Dear friends, since God so loved us, we also ought to love one another. (1 John 4:7–11)

WHAT WE MEAN BY SECURE LOVE

Because we were made in God's image,[1] we have built into our basic makeup an infinite capacity for love. Love starts at conception. Most moms, once they have found out that they are pregnant, begin to develop a love relationship with the baby inside them. Most children are received into arms of love when they are born.

But *desiring* to love your children and *actually* loving them in such a way that they develop a secure love of their own are two different things. You'd have to search a long time to find parents who would confess that they don't love their children. Almost all parents love their children, and children can find clear evidence of that love. But loving your child and even doing things to show your love do not translate into a *secure* love.

Let's define what we mean by secure love. This is a steady and sure love that is written on the hard drive of children's souls. It's a complete love that they default to when their hearts are under attack. It's the kind of love that children can confidently carry with them into the future.

We all long for a future that is kind to our children, but history has shown that tomorrow tends to take notes from yesterday. If the past is any indication, our children will certainly have their sense of being loved tested as they move into adulthood. They may have to function surrounded by personal hostility. The good news is that if we send them into the future armed with a secure love, they'll do just fine.

someday scenarios

Where will they be when they most need this secure love?

→ Maybe it will be when they're sitting across the table from someone they've given their heart to who has just told them that they don't love them anymore.

→ Maybe it will be when the bottom has fallen out of their financial world.

→ Maybe it will be when they hear two painful words: "You're fired!"

→ Maybe it will be when they've been set up and framed for something they didn't do.

→ Maybe it will be when they read a forwarded e-mail, and realize they've been betrayed by a friend.

→ Maybe it will be when they are standing beside a casket, holding the hand of their soul mate or one of the offspring from that union.

→ Maybe it will be when they are wearing a uniform, standing a lonely post, or facing a merciless enemy far from the safety of home.

These are scenarios in which you hope they will have the option to pick up a cell phone and call you, or maybe sit down at their computer and pour out their heart to you in an e-mail. But that's assuming they *can,* and it's also assuming you will be there to take that call or respond to that e-mail. As I said in the first chapter, our children are a gift we send to a time that we will not see. We need to send them into that time so secure that even if we have long since passed away, they will rest in the confidence that they are loved.

THE SECRET INGREDIENT

Here's the problem. In order to *feel* loved, you have to actually have someone directing his or her love toward you. You and I deeply love our children. If they should find themselves in an unloving scenario some day, we might be able to get in contact with them to remind them of how much we care. But what if we're dead? That will happen eventually, you know. They can't feel actual love from someone who no longer exists in their life, although the memory of our love can *comfort* them—maybe even inspire them. But that love will have a tough time *sustaining* them—especially if they are in a situation where their hearts are broken or are being mishandled. They need to know that the person who loves them is alive, well, and involved in their lives. I understand all that romanticized stuff people cling to. They believe that the loved ones who have passed on are somehow looking down from heaven and watching out for them. All of that may feel nice, but there is no biblical basis for assuming it's true.

> There is a love that we can pass on to them that is steady, sure, and available to them whether we are here or not, and I'm talking about the infinite love of God.

That sentimentality doesn't matter anyway. There is a love that we can pass on to them that is steady, sure, and available to them whether we are here or not, and I'm talking about the infinite love of God. This love can be transferred to them in a specific way and a general way. The specific way is when they receive God's love into their hearts by trusting in the hope found in the gospel. This not only puts the love of God into their hearts, it puts His Spirit there, too, as a permanent guest in their lives.

Keep in mind, however, that many children who give their hearts to God do not go into the future with a secure love. That kind of love may eventually find its place in their hearts as a result of personal growth and maturity in their faith, but for too many of them, it comes in the twilight of their lives. They miss out on its benefits for the lion's share of their adult years.

We can do something while our children are under our roof that significantly increases their capacity to move into their adult years with that mature and secure love firmly in place. This "general" transfer of love is the result of parents loving children the way God loves them. It's called grace.

aLL Love isn't created equaL

Before we go much further, we need to define what is meant by the word *love*. As I said earlier, you'd have a hard time finding a parent who doesn't dearly love his children. The reason many children move into adulthood insecure about love is not because their parents didn't love them, but because the love they received from their parents was incomplete.

→ **Sometimes our love is incomplete because our children feel they constantly have to compete for it.** We tell them we love them and then they watch us make decisions regarding our careers, our friends, or our pastimes that directly undermine our ability to invest the time in them that love requires. I heard about a son who felt that his father treated his hunting dogs better than he treated his kids. Here's the gist of what I heard about this father:

- He always went straight from his car to the dog pens to say hello to his dogs and pet them when he got home from work. When he came into the house, it was rare when they received a greeting from him.

- It was not uncommon for him to bring home treats for his dogs. When he spoke to them, it was always with a great deal of kindness and excitement in his voice. His kids never recalled a time when he spoke harshly to his dogs. But when it came to his children, he seldom had time to take them out for ice cream, but he could always find time to criticize them.

- He spent more time with his hunting dogs on weekends than with his kids. It wasn't that his kids didn't want to go hunting with their dad; he just didn't invite them.

- Sometimes they felt he even fed his dogs better than he did his own kids.

Careers can create a sense of competition for our children's hearts. Falling short in this area can transfer an incomplete and insecure love for them to take into the future. All of us have careers that demand a lot from us. We will always have to allocate more of our waking hours to our livelihoods than we do to anything or anyone else. That's simply the nature of careers, and kids understand that. But kids also know when we make deliberate choices to take something from them that they vitally need so we can enhance our careers. We communicate something that formats them with an insecure love. They don't question that we love them; they simply feel that we love other things *more*. We're talking about things that stroke our ego, fatten our paycheck, or soften our lifestyle. We might declare that we *have* to work as much

> But kids also know when we make deliberate choices to take something from them that they vitally need so we can enhance our careers.

as we do because of our bills, but then they see us deliberately making poor financial choices, which holds their lives hostage to the consequences.

> → **Sometimes our love is incomplete because our children feel like they have to earn it.** They figure out that they receive our praise and pride when they do things that make us look good or make our jobs as parents easier. These are kids who have to process a lot of guilt before they can find approval.

I know of a girl who is now a young mom. Back when she was little, she felt that love from the adults in her family always came with a price tag. Even her grandmother made her earn her love. She can remember from when she was around five years old through her teenage years how her grandmother would do something that constantly reminded her that she never measured up. For instance, she visited her grandmother weekly, which began with a hug. But when her grandmother hugged her, she would always place her hands on the sides of this girl's waist and pinch the skin. "You're getting a little chunky there, honey. You need to be careful of how much you eat."

This young woman got careful all right. Bulimia started running her life around thirteen years of age. One hundred thousand dollars in rehab and a set of false teeth later, this young mom feels like she's finally gotten her problem under control. She'll never feel like she's got it mastered, and to her dying day she'll always feel that bulimia is an unwelcome guest at every meal, but now she's got some semblance of health. Today, she's trying to do a better job with her own children than the adults in her life did with her.

It's easy for us to blame the way we love our kids on the way our parents loved us. So many parents today feel that they can't transfer the kind of secure love to their children that I'm describing here because their own parents failed to do this for them. Does that excuse us? Balanced minds would have to insist that it doesn't. It's an explanation, but it can't be used as a cop-out.

Love Defined

What helps us turn the cycle of incomplete love around is when we understand exactly what love is and what love requires. With that in mind, let me suggest a definition of love that can radically change your life. This definition of love can help you choose the right thing to do when dealing with your children. It helps you make hard choices and it encourages you when the cost of loving is high. Here's my definition:

> Love is the commitment of my will
> to your needs and best interests,
> regardless of the cost.

Let's walk through its three parts:

1. Love Is the Commitment of My Will . . .

In other words, doing the loving thing may not always come naturally to you. You may have to muster courage, say no to your fears, and place your feelings in check. Love is about making decisions based on the covenant we have with that person.

2. To Your Needs and Best Interests . . .

Not "to *my* needs and best interests." Love sees our needs as a "B" priority compared to the best interests of the person we are called to love. It is not in our children's best interest to give them everything they want, to make life easy for them, to side with them when they are clearly wrong, or to circumvent consequences for their sins. It is not in their best interests to facilitate false fears holding them hostage, to fight all their battles, or to rescue them from all their wrong choices. Love is about meeting their *actual* needs, not their selfish needs.

3. Regardless of the Cost

Secure love understands that loving someone is often inconvenient and sometimes painful. Loving your kids costs money, time, and sleep. It might cost a mom decades in time originally planned to be spent on her career. It might cost her her figure. It might cost a dad a promotion. It might mean that there are some amenities or lavish vacations you must do without. It definitely means eating crow, swallowing your pride, and asking for forgiveness a lot.

Many years ago I got my hair cut by a young woman named Peggy. She was a single woman in her mid-twenties—single but living with her boyfriend. She regularly moved our conversation to spiritual issues. It was obvious that her insecurities and the flawed views of love that often accompany insecurities were leading her to make decisions not in her best long-term interest. In spite of it all, she was always anxious to talk about the things of the heart.

Then Peggy got pregnant. She was delighted at the prospect of being a mom, and she even told me that this might be the thing her boyfriend needed to step up his commitment and marry her. During her pregnancy, I saw her on an average of once every three weeks. Each time I got my hair cut, we'd talk about the upcoming baby, parenting options, and building a strong family.

The big day came. I was scheduled to get a haircut by one of the other stylists. When I arrived, the women cutting my hair happened to be on the phone with Peggy, who was at the hospital. Crisis time: The baby was breech. The doctor wanted to do a C-section, but Peggy refused because she didn't want the scar. I asked to speak with her. She said her biggest concern was maintaining her figure after the baby was born. She had put on minimal weight and was certain that in a short period of time, she could have her original figure back. She told me, however, that she was certain the scar would be a turnoff to her boyfriend. She was afraid she'd be less appealing to him. I assured her that I was married to a woman who had had *four* C-sections, and each time my wife healed up just fine. The scar was barely noticeable, I said. That explanation wasn't good enough for Peggy. She was worried about losing what little she had—a cute body.

Her little boy was forced out backward. Serious damage was done to the leg sockets in his pelvis. He lived in a brace for the first eighteen months of his life. He's since grown past the injury and is walking fine, but once he hears and understands what really happened in the birthing room (secrets like this are almost impossible to keep),[2] he's going to have a hard time sensing the kind of "secure" love a parent is supposed to transfer. His mother's love is genuine but incomplete. She made her final decisions about him with her needs and best interests in front of his. Secure love has a price tag she wasn't willing to pay.

As I assumed would happen, her boyfriend hung around until the baby was born, and then he split the scene. So much for a scarless body.

making love secure

As you can see, saying that we love our children and doing certain things that communicate love isn't enough. We've got to love them in the way that God loves us—when they're unappreciative, when they don't deserve it, when it's inconvenient, when it is costly to us, even when it's painful.

There are three things that, done consistently, have a way of giving your children a sense of security that keeps them from doubting. It minimizes their need to search for the shallow love that the world system offers. It builds an authentic love in their hearts that ministers to them long after we are out of the picture. It takes so much of the allure out of the counterfeit love that Satan offers them.

1. Children feel secure when they know they are accepted as they are.

Let me qualify this before we clarify it. There are attitudes our children might develop that we never have to accept. Selfishness, disrespect, deceit, and any other sinful action does not have to be condoned or tolerated. Just as in our relationship with God, He may love us when we are sinful, but He doesn't ignore our sin. Just the opposite— He notices it. In Revelation 3:19 Jesus says, "Those whom I love I rebuke and discipline." God knows that if our sinful choices do not have consequences, they will destroy us. Because He loves us and doesn't want that to happen to us, He brings about consequences in our life that cause us to learn from our mistakes.

The "acceptance" I'm talking about is for those things that are part of our children's personal makeup. These are the unique things that make them individuals—the emotional, intellectual, and physical DNA. These are also the things that have no moral problems affixed to them. Many of our kids do things that annoy, frustrate, or embarrass us, but they are not wrong. Every time we point these things out, we tell them that they don't measure up. This builds a foundation of insecurity in them.

Boys are often berated because they are noisy, messy, or aggressive. Girls are often criticized for being too emotional, picky, or overly sensitive. Some kids are criticized for being slow, forgetful, or inquisitive, or for saying whatever pops into their heads. They have a hard time getting up, struggle in certain subjects in school, and are often taunted regarding physical features like their eyes, nose, teeth, neck, knees, feet, voice, hair texture, or their complexion.

Boys are criticized for liking girls; girls are criticized for liking boys. Some boys don't care for sports. Some girls don't like to play house. Teenagers require more sleep. Kids have always had their own way of communicating, their unique style of clothes and hair, and distinctive music. Kids go through awkward times where they don't think they're attractive, smart, or interesting. What is key in all of this is that a parent should communicate nothing but acceptance for the unique characteristics of their children. When they do that, a child senses the kind of acceptance that God has for us in our uniqueness.

Some girls know that their dads wish they had been born boys.

> What is key in all of this is that a parent should communicate nothing but acceptance for the unique characteristics of their children.

Some boys figure out that their mothers would rather have had girls. Kids hear when we lament how much work they are when they are little. Teenagers roll their eyes when we announce, "They're teens— what do you expect?" On the other hand, when they hear us say that it's an honor to have them in our home, that we are grateful for the chance to do all the things they need us to do for them (like haul them around, or spend a lot of money on them), they sense acceptance that makes them feel securely loved. Our attitude shouldn't be that we "have" to do all these things for them, but that we "get" to.

I was sitting in a hotel restaurant in Portland, Oregon. It was a Sunday morning. I was catching a plane around noon, which afforded me the luxury of enjoying a leisurely breakfast. This restaurant offered an all-inclusive breakfast buffet, with a lower price for kids.

A mom arrived with her two children: an infant and a boy approximately four years old. I noticed the boy right away. His face was filled with excitement, and his mouth was running a mile a minute as they circled the buffet line so that Mom could see the options. His mother held the infant while the boy followed along. He could barely contain his excitement. He saw the fruit, the varieties of cereal, the pancakes and waffles, and the station where the chef made omelets to your specifications. Then I watched his eyes pop out of his head as he studied the trays full of breakfast "desserts"—blueberry muffins, bear claws, and assorted Danish. This brief chance to watch this enthusiastic boy check out the breakfast buffet quickly became the highlight of my morning. I was watching a boy designed by God take a big breath out of every moment. He was absolutely in love with his surroundings. He looked like a boy who had gone to food heaven.

The hostess seated Mom and her two kids at the table directly across from me. The waitress filled their water glasses and asked if she could bring any coffee for the mother or juice for the kids. She asked if they were going to have the breakfast buffet.

"My husband will be down in a few minutes," the mother replied. "He and I are going to have the buffet. You can bring a bowl of cornflakes and some milk for my boy."

"Mom, no! I want to have the buffet, too!" the boy instantly responded. It was obvious that this boy had already mapped out his plan on how he was going to attack this buffet.

"You can't eat all that food. Most of it is just sugar. Forget it," the mom curtly said.

"But Mom, I *like* that kind of food, that's what I was *hoping* for. Please?" he pleaded.

"Forget it; you're not having the buffet, so hush up." She turned her back on the boy and started to tend to her infant.

"Ma'am, for just a dollar and a half more than the cornflakes, he could have the buffet," the waitress offered. She could see how anxious the boy was.

"No thanks. He doesn't need all of that food." The look on her face was a clear look of dismissal to the waitress.

As the mother preoccupied herself with her baby, I watched this young boy who had been so filled with excitement start to quietly turn into himself. And then the tears started. His anticipation and excitement had been stilted. I give the boy credit. He didn't cry out loud. He didn't argue, fuss, or make a scene. He just sat there and quietly hurt.

Dad arrived with the newspaper under his arm, sized up the situation, sat down in his chair and asked the boy why he was crying.

"I wanted to have the buffet, but Mom doesn't want me to."

He turned to his wife. "What's up? Why can't he have the buffet?"

She gave him the same practical and nutritional arguments she'd given the boy a few minutes earlier.

"Look, we're on vacation," Dad said. "He's never had an opportunity to do this before. The difference in cost is chump change. We can easily afford it. And as far as waste goes, what we don't eat they are most likely going to throw away."

There was a brief back-and-forth discussion before the mother gave in and agreed to let the boy have the buffet. His countenance immediately reverted back to that excited little boy who had made the initial review of the food stations. Within a minute, son and father were off to attack the buffet.

I had so much fun watching this boy go from station to station to get a little bit of everything. He saw people toast their bagels, so he did it, too. He could barely reach the toaster, but an older lady took joy in helping him work it. He got pancakes and a waffle and piled syrup and whipped cream on them. I loved the way he got in the omelet line, waited his turn, and then told the chef what he wanted, which was a little bit of everything. His final trips out were to the dessert station. I say trips because he made two. Before he was done, he had a sampling of each of the little desserts that had been laid out.

Meanwhile, Mom was feeding the baby, and Dad had taken a position at the table where he could spread out the Sunday paper. When the boy got all that he had been looking forward to having, he commenced to work his way through his breakfast feast. I was completely enjoying watching this little boy getting to experience this rare treat.

That's when Mom finally finished all feeding responsibilities of her infant and turned to study the various plates of food in front of her son.

And then she started.

"Why did you get both pancakes *and* waffles? And what's with all the whipped cream? You're just going to get that all over your clothes. And what's this on your bagel? Cream cheese? You've never had that before. Did you have any idea of what you were putting on this thing?"

She got her husband's attention. "Look at all of this. He even got an omelet."

She turned her attention back to the boy. "Why on earth did you order an omelet?" she demanded. "There is no way you can eat all of that." Pointing to the desserts, she said, "You get one, count 'em, *one* of these desserts. Pick the one you want because I'm going to take the other ones back. Why do you need a dessert anyway? It's breakfast, for crying out loud."

As she went through her diatribe, I watched the boy's countenance fall. This time it looked like a combination of helplessness and hopelessness. He tried to eat everything on the assorted plates, but his mother reminded him several times how foolish he had been for getting so much stuff. As promised, she took all but one of the desserts away from him and then berated her husband for not listening to her. Once she had adequately spoiled everyone's meal with guilt and condescension, she stood up and passed through the buffet line for herself. I just sat there and watched a little boy slowly eating his waffles, whipped cream coming out from the corners of his mouth, with tears streaming down his young face. By the time his mom got back, all the joy had drained from him.

Now I can hear what some are saying.

Waste.

Nutrition.

Sugar.

Kids can't get everything they want.

And don't forget, Tim, she had a little baby. She's tired. You don't know what that boy had been like earlier that morning. Maybe he had pushed her buttons to the brink. And it doesn't sound like her husband is much help.

I've heard it all over the years. I'm very aware of how strict, no-nonsense parents morally justify everything they do.

My questions are these: Was it worth it? Is that the way God treats us? Does God tease us with good things, insult us for being excited about them, and then scold us for trying to enjoy them? He's a God of grace who promised the children of Israel a land flowing with "milk and honey." David referred to Him as a shepherd and said that He causes us to lie down in green pastures and leads us beside the still waters. If you were a young, vulnerable sheep, you'd consider lush meadows of grass and quieted streams a lamb's buffet.

Eventually this little boy will grow up and become a young man

> Does God tease us with good things, insult us for being excited about them, and then scold us for trying to enjoy them?

heading out on his own. I don't doubt that he'll feel that his mother loved him, but unless she changes the way she's operating, he has little chance of leaving home with "secure" love—the kind of love that has registered on his heart that his parents enjoy him just the way he is.

Our daughter Karis was a busy child when she was little. She was easily distracted and lived her young years preoccupied with whatever was happening around her. In kindergarten, she would regularly shed her shoes. She liked her feet to be unencumbered and unconfined. When it was time for her class to line up to go to lunch or recess, her teacher would notice that she seldom had her shoes on. Karis was fortunate to have Ms. Civiliar as her kindergarten teacher because she didn't see Karis kicking off her shoes as a flaw. She didn't take it personally. She simply saw our daughter as one of those busy little children who shed her shoes because it made her somehow feel more comfortable in her first year of school.

Recently Karis, now married, had her first child—a girl. She brought her baby by her old elementary school, where Ms. Civiliar still taught kindergarten. Her former teacher went on and on about Karis's new baby. And then she said, "Karis, you know one of my fondest memories of you? It's how you would take off your shoes, and sometimes the class and I would work together to help you find them. I used to get such a kick out of that."

I used to get such a kick out of that. That's why Ms. Civiliar is such a wonderful teacher. She knows what is a problem and what isn't. She doesn't see these kinds of things as flaws, but just part of the nuances of a unique and special child. She sees them the way God sees them. I know of homes where Karis's habit of shedding her shoes would have been looked on as a *serious* problem:

"You need to be more organized."

"Why can't you remember something as vital as your shoes?"

"This is pure irresponsibility!"

"I don't want to see you taking off your shoes unless it's the end of the day."

These kinds of attitudes do not reflect the grace-filled heart of

God. When it comes to little boys who love buffets and little girls who do better in school with their shoes off, the bigger question is, "What difference does it make?"

The grace response is "None!" Grace's attitude is "Go for it!" or "I love it!" Having said this, I know there are times when children need to be told that they can't have the buffet or they need to keep their shoes on, but it shouldn't be an arbitrary thing. It should be times when it's *the only workable option* or makes *godly* sense. Otherwise, it makes no sense—especially if you are trying to treat your child the way God treats us. Kids inside homes where nonmoral issues are elevated to a level of *big* problems don't get to experience the kind of acceptance that makes a heart feel securely loved. Instead they live with a barrage of nitpicking criticism, receiving put-downs because they are curious, anxious, excited, helpless, carefree, or absent-minded.

There was a scene in Jesus' life in a public arena where children were trying to get close to Him. They were noisy and pushy as children will be, and the adults on the scene were doing their best to turn them away. Jesus saw what was going on and stopped the adults and parents from holding the children back.

Here's what He said:

Let the children alone, and do not hinder them from coming to Me; for the kingdom of heaven belongs to such as these. (Matthew 19:14 NASB)

When we receive our children as they are, we reflect the kind of love that God has for them. It's the kind of love that will carry them through the good times and the bad times for the rest of their lives.

2. Children feel secure when they know they are affiliated with a loving and honoring family.
Homes of honor.

It might seem like a pipe dream to you, but this is well within the grasp of people who view their fellow family members through a graceful set of eyes. Homes of honor see the other person's time, their gifts, their uniqueness, and their dreams as gifts to be cherished and stewarded. Homes of honor still have room for sibling rivalry. Homes of honor occasionally entertain arguments and disappointments, but for the most part, these homes give children a deep sense of being loved in a secure environment. All children are important, along with their opinions and concerns. Their time is respected, their ideas are respected, their space is respected, and their vulnerabilities are respected. There is a present-tense commitment to making each day an asset that builds on the day before.

The best way to see this become a reality among children is to make it the way parents deal with each other. I've even seen couples that have been through a divorce figure out how to deal with each other in honor and love even though the marriage didn't work out the way they'd hoped. Homes of honor understand forgiveness, they are committed to virtue, and they place high value on every individual in the circle.

> The righteous man leads a blameless life; blessed are his children after him. (Proverbs 20:7)

Scripture reminds us that the high regard we place on our reputation and the priority we place on treating the people close to us honorably will wash back over our children as blessings in their later life.

Everyone has favorite passages in the Bible. One of mine is the last part of Romans, chapter 8. Paul brings his powerful teaching on the grace of God to a crescendo. He talks of how grace helps us in our personal struggle with sin (Romans 7:7–25), how we can lead a victorious life through the power of God's Spirit (Romans 8:1–17), and of the future glory that awaits people who have taken part in the grace of God (Romans 8:18–27). Then it's as though he can't contain himself anymore, and he spills over with one of the most exciting passages of encouragement to people who have received the grace-filled love of God. A sampling reminds us of the secure love that awaits people who have allowed Christ to change their lives.

If God is for us, who can be against us? He who did not spare his own Son, but gave him up for us all—how will he not also, along with him, graciously give us all things? . . . In all these things we are more than conquerors through him who loved us. For I am convinced that neither death nor life, neither angels nor demons, neither the present nor the future, nor any powers, neither height nor depth, nor anything else in all creation, will be able to separate us from the love of God that is in Christ Jesus our Lord. (Romans 8:31b–32, 37–39)

Kids who live in a home where honor for each other rules the day grow up to be children with secure love tucked safely into their hearts.

3. Children feel secure love when they receive regular and generous helpings of affection.

Picture this: You've got some kind of itch in the middle of your back. It's out of the range of your arm, unless you're a contortionist. You look for a corner of a wall or a door to rub against to get some relief. Then a family member walks by, maybe your spouse or one of your children. They observe your dilemma. And then, with a few well-placed fingers on your back, relief washes all over you.

> Allow me to let you in on a secret. God has hard-wired our skin to our souls.

Why is it that when someone you love scratches your back, it always feels better than when you scratch your back yourself? Allow me to let you in on a secret. God has hard-wired our skin to our souls. Somehow, He saw fit to configure our outer covering to be one of the greatest tools for transferring a sense of secure love.

Everyone was designed to respond to affection. With rare exceptions, children are especially responsive to meaningful, tender touch. The hugs and kisses they receive from their parents from the moment they are born create a reservoir of security in their hearts. Both genders need it from both parents. Sons and daughters fare far better if they receive plenty of lap time from their moms *and* dads. They sleep better at night when their parents have stopped by their rooms to tell them how much they love them, to pray over them, and to kiss them good night.

That type of parental love shouldn't stop as they move into the teenage years. Obviously, strapping young boys and maturing girls may be too big to hold on your lap. And they might be self-conscious about receiving affection from you in front of their friends. Some might even go through a stage where they turn away from you when you try to hug them or kiss them, but they still need meaningful touch. It might be a hand on their shoulder, a playful punch on the arm, or some wrestling in the pool. They still need touch, and deep down in their hearts, they want it. They want to know that someone isn't ashamed or afraid to touch them. It's a crucial gift they need at a time in their lives when many feel unattractive and untouchable.

Did you ever have a famous person visit your house when you were young? Now imagine what it must be like for a child to stand in the background when, say, Michael Jordan drops by. The world's most famous basketball player isn't there to visit the child, and the child assumes that he's invisible to a person with such immense fame. Wouldn't the effect be profound if, out of all the faces in that gathering, the celebrity would actually call the child, put him on his lap, and make him the center of attention?

That's exactly what Jesus did after a long, demanding day. On the trip to Capernaum, Jesus' disciples had been arguing over which one of them was going to be the greatest in the kingdom of God. They had retired to a private home, and after they got settled, Jesus asked them what they had been arguing about. Once they told Him, He decided to show them who really is the greatest in the kingdom of heaven. Look at how Mark relayed the account:

Taking a child, He set him before them, *and taking him in His arms*, He said to them, "Whoever receives one child *like this* in My name receives Me . . ." (Mark 9:36–37a NASB, emphasis mine)

Notice that He took the child in His arms. This was without doubt one of the most fortunate children in all history. He actually got to sit in the lap of God and feel God's arms around him. Jesus loves children. They represent the attitude of heaven. This child showed immediate obedience and was simply glad to be loved. It didn't matter to him which disciple got the biggest chair once they got to heaven. He was enjoying the gentle touch of his Savior right here on earth.

Jesus said that when we receive children as He does, it's not only showing love to the child but also to God, who made the child. He said, ". . . whoever receives one child *like this*." What did he mean by "like this"? He could have meant in the way He received that *particular* boy, but if that were indeed what He meant, it would rule out girls, kids at different ages, and kids with different physical features. Most likely, when He said "like this," He was referring to the affectionate and tender way He was holding the boy.

Jesus understood the power of affection in communicating secure love. Healthy, meaningful touch toward our sons and daughters makes it easy for them to give and receive affection as adults. It also gives them a clear sense of the counterfeit that masquerades as affection. It helps them to transfer the legacy of love they have received from you to the next generation in your family tree.

DIFFICULT, BUT NOT IMPOSSIBLE

If they're forming a line for parents who have fallen short, and you feel that you should be in it, you'll have to get in line behind me. We've all fallen short. We may not have pulled a scene like the mother at the buffet, but we've stolen our children's joy unnecessarily more times than we'd like to count. We've turned nonissues into crises. We've sculpted molehills into mountains. We've reached inside our children's hearts and pinched them simply because we could.

God is in the forgiveness business. He loves to get out the sponge and clean the chalkboard filled with the marks that have accumulated against us. Sure, He has to use blood instead of water to wash away our sins. And, yes, the blood is from His only precious Son, but everything was worth it to Him because *you* were worth it. God loves you more than you can ever know. He loves you just as you are. He wants you to enjoy your good standing in His personal Home of Honor. He wants to put His arm around you and pull you close to His heart.

> If you're like me, you need to hear Him say, "It's all right. I forgive you. I'll help you recover from the mistakes you've made with your kids."

If you're like me, you need to hear Him say, "It's all right. I forgive you. I'll help you recover from the mistakes you've made with your kids." Ask Him to forgive you. Ask Him to help you meet this driving inner need of your child. Tell Him how much you want to pass on to your child not only love, but a secure love that can go with him all the way through his life. He's a forgiver. That's what He's all about.

One more thing: You might need to ask your children's forgiveness, too. You need to let them know that you recognize you've failed them, that you've hurt them, and that at times you've stolen their joy. Be specific. Even if you have to go back years, let them know that you know you were wrong. It doesn't make you smaller in their eyes. In fact, it makes you just the opposite. In your humble contrition, you will demonstrate something they desperately need if they want to have a love that is secure—grace.

> Above all, love each other deeply, because love covers over a multitude of sins. Offer hospitality to one another without grumbling. Each one should use whatever gift he has received to serve others, faithfully administering God's grace in its various forms. (1 Peter 4:8-10)

And don't be surprised if you find yourself overwhelmed with the urge to offer acceptance, affiliation, and affection to your children on a daily basis. These are three gifts that keep on giving . . . long after you are gone.

CHAPTER 4

a SIGNIFICANT PURPOSE

Every once in a while, a story slips out Hollywood's back door that out-teaches the best Sunday school lesson and out-inspires the most eloquent sermon. *October Sky* was such a movie.

The year was 1957. The place was Coalwood, West Virginia. The setting defined the dilemma. Coalwood was a coal-mining town breathing its last few gasps of black dust before it would shut down for good. The mine that had sustained generations of Coalwood families was starting to give out. The owners of the mine were trying to get more for less. The union was fighting to keep what little they had. Caught in the middle was the project foreman, who was trying to keep both sides from giving up or destroying each other. Coalwood needed a touch of grace.

It was a town defined by a dark hole in the ground. If you were a young man growing up in Coalwood, it was assumed you'd end up down in the mine. If you were a young girl, you'd marry one of those miners and raise his boys to someday take his place. Like a magnet that pulled them in, few felt they had a chance of escaping the coal miner's life.

But one autumn night, something appeared in the October sky that forced the people of Coalwood to take their focus off the ground long enough to look up. The Soviet Union had put the first orbiting satellite into space. The race for the outer reaches of Earth's gravity had begun. During one of the darkest chapters of the Cold War, a Soviet satellite named *Sputnik* threatened to tip the scales in the fight for political and military superiority toward the Russians. The assumption was that whoever owned space would ultimately dominate the world.

To the townsfolk, the light streaking across the sky some twenty-five thousand miles away was met with a sense of gloom and defeat. Over the decades these people had been programmed to think small. Working in the darkness and danger of the mine had jaded their capacity to dream. "Hope" seldom appeared in their minds in capital letters.

But in the background of that huddled group of townspeople, standing in the silhouettes of those mighty miners, was a young boy who saw *Sputnik* as the opportunity he had been waiting for. Homer Hickam had seen what the mine could do to a man. He'd watched it turn his father into a walking candidate for black lung. He'd seen how it treated a marriage and punished children. It was Homer's father who was that foreman trying to keep the town alive. His father was a single-minded man whose life was dictated by demands of that black hole.

The mine had turned his father into a graceless, angry man— blinded him as well. The father couldn't see what it was doing to his boy. He couldn't overcome his myopic view of the future to see the potential in his son to do something more—something greater. Homer knew that his father assumed he would someday follow him down the elevator into the bowels of the earth. The young man knew he was expected to surrender all his dreams to the fossil fuel that ruled the town. Because of whose son he was, there was even talk that he might inherit his father's position as the point man of the operation. But Homer wanted none of it. It wasn't because of his disdain for the mine or because of any disrespect for his father, but rather his belief that he was put on the earth for something different—something strategic.

That's what pushed Homer Hickam to convince two friends and an unpopular bookworm from school to help him chase the moon and reach for the stars. These four boys became obsessed with learning all they could about rocketry. Using their limited resources and their abundant ingenuity, they turned a nearby slag dump into a launch pad for their series of rockets. Encouraged by one of their high-school teachers, they parlayed their interest into a quest to win a national science competition. Homer was also inspired by the NASA legend Dr. Wernher von Braun. And even though they built one failure after another, this quartet's desire for something great demanded that they not give up.

But Homer's dreams of using his gifts to reach out into the unknowns of space only increased the distance between him and his father. It magnified the tension between them, too. His father's disappointment cut deep, and his lack of participation in Homer's rocket launches, even after the town had made it a community affair, broke his son's heart. Homer longed for the grace that applauded dreams and developed potential.

October Sky resonates with audiences because it portrays the pain that

October Sky resonates with audiences because it portrays the pain that so many children go through in search of their purpose.

so many children go through in search of their purpose. There is a deep longing in the heart of every child to "make a difference." They were hard-wired by God to want to do more than take up space and suck up air. They weren't born to be common denominators or mere faces in the crowd. That's why tyrannical governments get so little out of their people. God didn't create us to ignore our potential or abandon our dreams. He meant for us to be free so that we could pursue our potential with abandon. Despots, and the oppression that often accompanies them, insult God by refusing to create the environment that encourages potential to take root and grow.

Tyrannical families blunt potential, too. So do preoccupied families and indifferent families and lazy families. Our children deserve better. God has left us as stewards of our children's gifts and skills. Just as God has given us a chance to send our children into the future with a secure love, He has also given us the opportunity to send our children into the future with a significant purpose.

ACCIDENTAL DIVINITY?

God is a God of deliberateness. He does nothing by trial and error. His creation was not a series of chance accidents. From the moment He said, "Let there be light" (Genesis 1:3), He has been demonstrating that He is working a Big Plan. He sent His Son with a clearly defined purpose. Scripture says:

> Therefore, when Christ came into the world, he said: "Sacrifice and offering you did not desire, but a body you prepared for me; with burnt offerings and sin offerings you were not pleased. Then I said, 'Here I am—it is written about me in the scroll—I have come to do your will, O God.'" (Hebrews 10:5–7)

One of the highlights of His plan was when He said, "It is finished" (John 19:30). Not only does it illustrate the overwhelming sense of purpose that God brings to His relationship with mankind, it shows to what extent He's willing to go to achieve it. He's been involved in every aspect of mankind's history, and He left an entire book behind in the Bible that outlines His purposes and plans for our future.[1]

Along the timeline of history, God has used people with purpose as partners in His Big Plan. As a result of being made in His likeness,[2] we have a gnawing need to matter. It's a sense of purpose that comes from being one of His created works of art. He meant these purposes to be developed and realized. Although many people can contribute to this process, it is the child's parents that carry the greatest potential for influence. We're the ones who donated (in most cases) the basic ingredients for their DNA. We're the ones who were given the naming rights. We're the ones who invest most of the time and put up most of the money toward our children's best interests. That makes us the best candidates for grooming the limitless creativity God has built into their lives. It also places us in the default position of being the single most influential obstacle to our children's developing a significant purpose.

WHY aRe We HeRe?

Years ago, I worked in an office that had a poster of the Milky Way galaxy in the lunchroom. Just a little off center and down toward the right of this telescopic photo of millions of stars was a small caption box with an arrow pointing to a speck of dust. Inside the box were the words "You are here."

That's how we feel sometimes. We're stuck in the middle of the vast expanse of life, and we wish we could isolate our whereabouts a little better. The power of a secure love tells you where you are. You are ground zero in the middle of God's grace, surrounded by a caring and honoring family that accepts you. They communicate that love through meaningful touch, encouraging words, and sacrificial actions.

What helps that secure love gain maximum "relational market share" is when we can also answer the age-old question that philosophers have asked since the beginning of time: "Why am I here?" A significant purpose does that.

one WaY oR THe oTHeR

Here's what's interesting: If we fail to address our children's need for a significant purpose, it doesn't mean they will necessarily end up living useless and unproductive lives. In most cases, our lack of deliberateness in grooming their sense of purpose sends them into the future with a foreboding sense of irrelevancy and far more vulnerable to Satan's counterfeits.

There are exceptions, though, Homer Hickam being one of them. He pursued his dreams in spite of his father's antagonism. He ended up earning the right degrees and joining NASA as part of the team that sent dozens of crews of astronauts into space through the space shuttle program. One factor that stirred him on was the change of heart his father ultimately had about Homer's love of space. Many children who have been brought up in horrific homes can still end up making terrific contributions to society as adults. Some, however, never *feel* they are making a difference or feel they have *permission* to enjoy the fulfillment of their grand purposes. The fact is that without a parent's deliberate and gracious involvement in identifying and developing potential, children can go into adulthood with a scarred purpose. Let me list some examples:

1. An Underdeveloped Purpose

Without the grace to see our children as youngsters with great gifts, many kids proceed into adulthood with an unclear purpose. Sometimes it's an undeveloped purpose that never comes close to its capabilities. These are the kids who tried their hands at different options—sports, academics, drama, service, and church—until they found something that felt right. They sought affirmation from their parents only to find them preoccupied or disinterested. Often these children grow into adults who seldom feel like they measure up to their parents' expectations. Regardless of their contribution to society, these children grow old sensing that what they did with their life made little difference.

2. A Revengeful Purpose

When parents fail to carefully groom a child's sense of purpose, many of these children pursue a path designed to get even with their folks.

It's part "I'll show you" and part "Take that!" This especially happens when the parents have deliberately worked to undermine the development of their sense of purpose. They told their children that they were stupid, or uncoordinated, or too gangly to achieve success in a certain career.

3. A Wasted Purpose

Some young people are set up by their parents to pursue goals that never come close to tapping their potential. Homer Hickam would have made a fine coal miner, but it would have been the equivalent of using an F-16 to crop-dust. (I'm not in any way trivializing the role of a coal miner. I was born in western Pennsylvania, and my grandfather was a coal miner. It's a noble profession that renders a tremendous service for the common good, but it does-n't require extensive education, advanced mathematics, or much creativity.) There were many men in Homer Hickam's town who could be trained to harvest the coal out of the ground, but there was probably only one man in Coalwood who could be trained to help send men and women into outer space. Many young people never find their niche because they don't have parents who are willing to help them hunt for it.

> Many young people never find their niche because they don't have parents who are willing to help them hunt for it.

Robert Lewis summarizes his arguments for building a "transcendent cause" into your child in his book *Raising a Modern-Day Knight*. In driving home the sad point of a wasted purpose, he writes, "Nothing grates on a man's spirit quite like irrelevance. The knowledge that our best efforts and heroic deeds were meaningless is a bitter pill to swallow."[3]

It makes you wonder how many home runs were never hit, how many new products were never invented, how many songs were never written, or how many elections were never won. Untapped potential is a crime to humanity, an insult to God, and a shame for an individual. We can make sure this is never a consequence for our children or an indictment on us.

LET'S GO BACK TO THE MOVIES

Glenn Holland was a reluctant schoolteacher. He had taken a job as a band director at a local high school as a way of paying the bills while he wrote his "opus." He prided himself as a composer, and he wished he could spend the hours of his day sitting at his baby grand piano developing the different movements to his symphony. But first-time composers have a hard time putting food on the table, which is what caused him to end up in front of a roomful of unfocused and undisciplined musicians. The Hollywood film *Mr. Holland's Opus* is a fictional account of what happens in reality when teachers take their job seriously. This movie was a celebration of the power of influence on human potential. Glenn Holland, played by Richard Dreyfuss, didn't see the stewardship he had been given until he shifted from viewing his students as a means to a paycheck to seeing them as individuals who longed to be groomed for greatness.

There is a scene early in the story where we are introduced to a girl named Gertrude Lang. She's a forgettable member of the student body struggling to master the clarinet. Mr. Holland offers to give her some individual attention, but he grows annoyed and impatient with her lack of improvement. Her best efforts yield a series of squeaks. When he abruptly dismisses her, she sees this as his summary of her potential as a musician and decides to give up trying to master such a challenging instrument. But her resignation comes with tears. She was hoping that she could find something—one thing at least—that she could be good at.

When Mr. Holland inquires about the tears, Gertrude explains the pain of being an average girl in a family of overachievers. "My sister's got a ballet scholarship to Julliard," she says. "My brother is going to Notre Dame on a football scholarship; my mother has won the blue ribbon for watercolors at the state fair so much they retired the category; and my father has a beautiful voice."[4] When Glenn Holland finally sees what was always there—a human being longing to develop her potential—he decides to put his heart into turning this girl into an accomplished clarinetist. By graduation day, Gertrude has developed her skills well enough to play a brief solo as the orchestra performs for the parents.

Mr. Holland's Opus is not just a story about the power of a teacher's influence; it's also an illustration of the potential impact of a parent. Our children's teachers play a huge and strategic role in their lives. Their effectiveness is far more contingent on our influence than we'd like to admit, though. In the bigger scheme of life, it is more important that we help our children reach their potential than it is to see our own dreams come true. Many parents aren't willing to make that sacrifice, but those who are often find that they gain much more in the end.

That's the message of this movie. In the final scene of *Mr. Holland's Opus*, Glenn Holland is forced into retirement as a result of budget cuts to the music department. As he's walking down the hallway for one last time, ready to exit the school he's taught at all of his life, he hears a commotion in the auditorium. When he looks in, he sees it filled with thousands of students, staff, and alumni who have gathered to thank him for his contribution to their lives. Unbeknownst to him, his wife has made copies of his *Opus*. The orchestra that has assembled for this event is made up of present and former band members who have rehearsed his opus to a level of perfection.

Making a grand entrance at the last minute is one of his former students, now the governor of the state, Gertrude Lang. She takes the podium to pay tribute to Mr. Holland's years of sacrifice, hands him a conductor's baton, and then takes her place in the clarinet section. That's when Glenn Holland, overwhelmed with emotion, lifts his baton and begins conducting this orchestra in the first public performance of the *Opus* he had been working on since the beginning of his career as a band teacher. The symphony that he's felt in his heart, but only heard in his head, now fills the ears of the people he has served all of his adult life.

There are many sub-points to this stirring story, but one stands out that is vital to our discussion on transferring a significant purpose to our children: It's not so much the specific skills we help our children develop that guarantee their future greatness, but rather what those skills enable them to become. It's doubtful that Gertrude Lang became the governor of the state because of her ability as a clarinetist, but it was the sense of achievement in that area that spurred her to other accomplishments, such as becoming a great leader. So it is with our investment in our children's lives.

Layers of Potential

Our children were born with a need to find a purpose in life, and there are several levels in which that purpose needs to be found.

1. A General Purpose

Some basic things enable your children to play a strategic role in the larger family of man. Teaching them the benefit of putting higher value on others than they do on themselves empowers them to look out for the weak and disenfranchised people they encounter each day. Scripture says, "Do nothing out of selfish ambition or vain conceit, but in humility consider others better than yourselves. Each of you should look not only to your own interests, but also to the interests of others" (Philippians 2:3–4). Showing them the benefit of hard work turns them into a lifelong asset rather than a daily liability. St. Paul says, "Make it your ambition to lead a quiet life, to mind your own business and to work with your hands, just as we told you, so that your daily life may win the respect of outsiders and so that you will not be dependent on anybody" (1 Thessalonians 4:11–12).

One of the great general purposes you can transfer to your children is the goal of being a *wisdom hunter*. Wisdom is seldom available to the young, but it's made available sooner rather than later when we see that part of our role as parents is to teach our children how to turn knowledge into practical truth and insight. That's all wisdom is—knowledge with the ability to utilize it effectively. The prerequisite for a wisdom hunter is an overriding fear of God. While fearing God doesn't give you wisdom, it does give you the keys to the corridor that leads to it.[5] Sociologist Allan Bloom has put his hand on the pulse of this issue. Read carefully what he says:

> Fathers and mothers have lost the idea that the highest aspiration they might have for their children is for them to be wise—as priests, prophets or philosophers are wise. Specialized competence and success are all that they [most fathers and mothers] can imagine.[6]

Leaving the world nicer than you found it, making a commitment to a lifetime of learning, paying attention to what you learn from life's experience so that you are more valuable to others, and being committed to developing the potential of as many people as you can are general purposes that are good to install in the hearts of each one of your children. When they step into adulthood with these qualities as part of their character, they feel significant. By the way, it's really not that difficult to build these purposes into your kids. You simply develop these general purposes in your own life. Children embrace what is modeled far more than what they are told. Our good advice carries clout only when it is consistent with our example. As our children notice these wonderful qualities in us, it will be far easier for them to make them their own.

2. A Specific Purpose

God has given everyone certain skills and abilities. Sometimes they are obvious. You might have a musical prodigy or the next Tiger Woods. With little prodding they find that God has imbued them with a sophisticated and highly developed skill. These kinds of children pose a challenge for parents. Because they are so good at one thing, it is easy to let them slide in other areas. That's a mistake. One of the worst things we can do for our children is to send them into their adult years as a one-dimensional person. The accolades they receive in their area of skill cannot offset the rejection they'll receive in the other crucial dimensions of their life that were never developed. Many extraordinary athletes and entertainers struggle with this dilemma.

Most likely, you won't have to deal with the happy problem of raising a prodigy. The standard challenge of a grace-based parent is to help your children develop a workable skill in most areas of their lives and a highly disciplined skill in the area of their giftedness. When we make it our goal to notice their talent and then build structure around those talents, we set our children up to enjoy a significant purpose as part of their lifestyle.

3. A Relational Purpose

God has not designed humans to live as islands; disconnected from the people and places around them. A significant purpose assumes a working knowledge of the things that encourage relationships to grow deeply. In this regard, wise parents teach their children how to love, how to be forthright, how to be transparent with close friends, how to confront, and how to forgive. All that said, it must be added that building a significant purpose into your children invariably guarantees that some people *won't like them*. People of purpose annoy—even infuriate—those who want to coast through life.

> People of purpose annoy— even infuriate— those who want to coast through life.

Also, a relational purpose grounded on absolute morality will threaten people who want to redefine morals as their circumstances dictate. Children need to be forewarned that living a purposeful life has a way of bringing out the worst in some folks today. But they need to be assured that the benefits of treating people properly almost always outweigh the reactions.

As author Reuben Welch said, "I discovered that as I began to love people and care for people and become more involved with people, I had more joy, more life, more tears, more laughter, more meaning, and far greater fun than I ever had before."[7]

4. A Spiritual Purpose

It's amazing how many parents will pour decades of intense effort into developing their children's general purposes, specific purposes, and even their relational purposes, but completely ignore the spiritual dimension. It's as though they don't even recognize that it exists.

Some don't.

Ignorance of its existence doesn't absolve them from the responsibility of addressing it, and denial of its existence doesn't somehow magically make it disappear. The spiritual dimension of the human heart is as real and relevant as the physical, intellectual, and emotional dimensions. A decent parent wouldn't think of withholding food from his children. Children have physical needs that require daily nourishment to live. A decent parent wouldn't think of withholding knowledge and education from his children. Children are intellectual. Being kept illiterate handicaps their potential. A decent parent wouldn't think of withholding encouragement, kindness, and affection from his children. Children are emotional; they can cry and laugh and feel. Their emotions require daily care to keep them balanced.

In the same way, children *are* spiritual. Their spiritual dimension is just as real as any of the other three dimensions. Yet some parents, through their ignorance or denial of its existence, leave their children starved, illiterate, and unhealthy when it comes to spiritual matters.

Legendary artist Bob Dylan has a way with words. When he steps up to a microphone, he not only brings one of the most original voices in rock-'n'-roll to the forefront, but he also brings songs packed with pathos, poetry, and power. He summed up this point I'm trying to make in a song he wrote for his *Slow Train Coming* album.[8] Each verse keeps up a litany of options that lead to the same conclusion. Let me give you a sample:

You may be an ambassador to England or France.
You might like to gamble; you might like to dance.
You might be the heavyweight champion of the world.
You might be a socialite with a long string of pearls,
But you're gonna have to serve somebody.
Yeah, you're gonna have to serve somebody.
It may be the devil, or it may be the Lord,
But you're gonna have to serve somebody.

We've got to make sure we get Dylan's point. Your children have two choices and *only* two choices. They can give their lives to the Lord or *not give* their lives to the Lord. But if they choose not to, they—by default—are handing that area over to the forces of evil. Neutrality is not an option. No one is the captain of his or her own ship or the master of his or her own fate. That's one of the poetic lies that has been believed for too long. Parents who want to raise their children with grace must embrace the assumption that their children *are* spiritual.

Here's the rub: Many parents who don't question their children have a spiritual dimension believe it's something the child has to figure out on his or her own. That was the case of John Walker Lindh—"Johnny Jihad." As you may recall, John was picked up in the early days of the Afghanistan conflict following 9/11 when he was fighting with the Taliban. The young man, gifted intellectually, was raised in Marin County, California. I don't question that his parents loved him, but as we've already established earlier, some parents' love is incomplete. In the case of John Walker Lindh's *spiritual* purpose, this seems to be the case.

One of his parents was kind of a Catholic; the other was kind of a Buddhist. They encouraged John's intellectual and relational pursuits. When it came to meeting his driving inner need for purpose, as well as his inner need for love and hope, he was left on his own. The outcome was tragic. John Walker Lindh longed for a significant spiritual purpose. Radical Islam stepped into the void and offered him an answer to what his heart longed for.

Then the terrorists struck the World Trade Center and the Pentagon on September 11. Shortly after this horrific event, we sent our troops to Afghanistan to stab the heart of the terrorist network that caused the attack. We didn't expect to find a misdirected teenager from Marin County fighting with the Taliban. When our military forces captured John Walker Lindh, he was a visible example of what parental neglect of a spiritual purpose can lead to. His time with the Taliban and his training at the hands of Osama bin Laden had scarred him inside and out. That's because when it comes to spiritual issues, everybody is going to have to serve *somebody*. It may be the devil or it may be the Lord, or, as it was in John Lindh's case, it may be Islamic *jihad*. For the bulk of John Walker Lindh's remaining life, he'll get to reflect on his choice from inside the cage of a federal prison. What a shame. It didn't have to turn out like this.

Entire books have been written on how to develop a spiritual purpose. The point of this book is not to exhaust this issue but to prioritize it. Our children are deeply loved by God. He wants to have a meaningful and eternal relationship with them. He wants that relationship to enable them to live a life that makes a spiritual difference. Let me grab my "broad brush" and give you a couple of verses that outline some of the parameters of a significant spiritual purpose:

> He has showed you, O man, what is good. And what does the LORD require of you? To act justly and to love mercy and to walk humbly with your God. (Micah 6:8)

In a world so thirsty for grace, people who act justly, love mercy, and walk humbly make such a huge difference. They are people who wake up each day with a significant purpose.

> You are the salt of the earth . . . You are the light of the world . . . Let your light shine before men, that they may see your good deeds and praise your Father in heaven. (Matthew 5:13, 14, 16)

Seasoning is like grace for our food. Bland meals come alive when we sprinkle the right touch of spice. God wants us to send our children into the future equipped to offer that touch of grace to the people around them. He wants them to be the salt of the *earth*. In other words, God wants us to equip our children so that they leave our homes with such a clear spiritual purpose that it can add the right touch to whatever part of the world they may wander to.

Light is like grace in the darkness. It's amazing how much more comfortable we feel in the darkness when we have just enough light to see by. Children equipped to radiate God's grace take the edge off the people around them. And like salt, God has called them to be lights that light up the entire *world*. They can. It just takes our instilling a significant spiritual purpose in their hearts.

One of the greatest proofs that God has built a sense of purpose in us can be gleaned from Jesus' parable of the talents. In this clever story, Jesus talks about three people who were given different amounts of money and encouraged by their master to handle the money well. It is key that we take in the big picture of this parable. *None* of the money belonged to these servants. It belonged to their master. They were merely given the money and encouraged to handle it carefully.

> Children equipped to radiate God's grace take the edge off the people around them.

The one given the least amount did nothing with it. He didn't invest it, or leverage it, or even put it in a bank where it could have at least earned interest. He buried the talent given to him. When the master showed back up in his life, he was infuriated with this man for having nothing to show for his efforts. The consequences for his unwillingness to harness the potential of what he was given were severe.

The two other servants were given different amounts of money. With diligence and shrewdness, each managed to double what they had started with. They were able to give back to the master far more than he had originally given them. Look at what the master says to them:

> Well done, good and faithful servant! You have been faithful with a few things; I will put you in charge of many things. Come and share your master's happiness! (Matthew 25:21)

BUILDING SIGNIFICANT PURPOSE IN YOUR CHILD

The God of purpose has built an inner need for significance into each one of our children. They were born with it and long to have it developed into something that makes their lives significant. Let me conclude this chapter by giving you three things that you can do to help build this significant purpose into your child.

1. Children feel significant when they are regularly affirmed.

There is a cause and effect between encouragement and confidence. Kids who hear well-timed and well-placed affirmation from their parents are more easily convinced of the truth the Bible says about their intrinsic worth. David spent an entire psalm developing the reality of this value, which God has built within each of us. He says in Psalm 139:

> I will give thanks to Thee, for I am fearfully and wonderfully made; wonderful are Thy works, and my soul knows it very well. (v. 14 NASB)

When we affirm our children, we are validating this truth. It's a combination of positively confirming their worth and voicing our dedication to them as our children. We need to consistently do this in all the dimensions we mentioned above—physically, intellectually, emotionally, and spiritually. Kids brought up in an environment of legitimate praise build a solid resistance against the insults and put-downs that often bombard them from culture.

It's easy, however, to slip over a thin line and offer unfounded praise. This is done when we applaud them for something they aren't responsible for or overstate their contribution to some effort they've made. The parents who do backflips for the young child who just slid down a playground slide might mean well, but they might be setting their child up for some frustration.

I remember a particular couple who were playing with their son during a lunch break from work. They had picked him up at his day-care center, and they were obviously trying to pack a lot of compliments into the fifteen minutes they had to play with him. Perhaps they felt guilty. I'm not sure. But Dad would climb the ladder of the slide with the toddler hanging over his arm, place him on the slide, and shove him over the incline. Down he'd go to the waiting arms of his mother. This was fine. But the show they put on each time he did this made me wonder if they weren't setting this kid up to thrive on false praise.

While Dad stood at the top of the ladder clapping and whistling, Mom would lift the little boy into her arms and say things like, "You are the best slider in the whole park. There's no one I know who can slide as good as you. I'm so proud of how brave you are. You are the bravest boy I know." This went on and on. I don't doubt that the boy liked what he heard, but none of it was true. He wasn't a slider; he was an object of the law of gravity. His father was setting him at the top of a steep, slick, polished metal hill and pushing him over the edge. *Anybody* in this same scenario would zip down to the bottom. This little boy wasn't brave either. He had no choice but to end up at the bottom of the incline.

This might seem like a petty example to you, but it is this kind of graceless and empty complimenting that sets a child up for serious heartache when he finds himself among other children who legitimately earn praise. It also gives him inner conflict when the appraisal from more objective people in his childhood (like teachers, coaches, and friends) comes in far less complimentary. Parents who throw around empty praise often attack people in their children's lives who assess them accurately.

If this boy's parents had said things like, "Wow, I love the look in your eyes as you fly down the slide. You look so excited," or "I love to play with you like this. It's fun watching you go down the slide," they would be verbalizing accurate observations. They could have affirmed his courage if he had been reluctant to climb the ladder to the top but did it anyway. But they didn't even give him the opportunity to climb the ladder—even though he wanted to try. They were afraid he might fall (we'll address this problem in the next chapter).

Affirmation catches your children doing things right. It notices when they do things you know don't come easy to them. It applauds them when they fix a wrong or dig themselves out of a hole they've made (like bringing up a poor grade). It thanks them for living out their moral principles and being willing to stand alone for their convictions.

There are things we can do that nullify our affirmation. If we view our children as burdens, make statements about how much more difficult they've made our lives, or remind them of how little freedom we have now that they've come along, we're saying, "You lack value. You're not important enough to me."

Another thing that really undermines our ability to develop a significant purpose in them happens when we pass on all those negative comments about teenagers. When we ridicule, mock, or insult their age group in general or them in particular, we're communicating that they are fundamentally flawed. This comes at a time when they naturally think that of themselves anyway. Teenagers tend to be overly self-conscious. When we fan that flame, we can put impressions in their minds that have the potential of diminishing their sense of significance for the rest of their lives. Too many parents unwittingly communicate to their teenagers that they are annoyed and inconvenienced by this corridor they are passing through.

> The teenage years are some of the most exciting years of parenting.

85

The teenage years are some of the most exciting years of parenting. When parents are fearful of this stage of their children's development, it causes the children to be reluctant to trust them, or to turn to them when they are confused, or to confide in them when they are carrying a heavy burden. This is also a time when parents should be putting the finishing touches on their general, specific, relational, and spiritual purposes. (Don't worry if you feel you've already blown it—later in this chapter we'll see that it's never too late.) They need to know that they have a parent they can count on. This does wonders in transferring the sense of significance they need to take into the future.

2. Children feel significant when they know they have our attention.

Jesus noticed kids. He was notorious for looking past all the adults crowding around Him to draw attention to some child on the fringe. You see Him do this in Matthew 18. Not only does He give His attention to this child, He offers a sobering warning to adults who don't pay careful attention to children's needs. Look at what He says:

> Whoever receives one such child in My name receives Me; but whoever causes one of these little ones who believe in Me to stumble, it is better for him that a heavy millstone be hung around his neck, and that he be drowned in the depth of the sea . . . See that you do not despise one of these little ones, for I say to you, that their angels in heaven continually behold the face of My Father who is in heaven. (Matthew 18:5–6, 10 NASB)

If God thinks it's important for the angels in heaven to pay attention to the details of our children's lives, how much more would He expect from their parents? We need to have a working knowledge of our children's likes and dislikes, their friends and their detractors, and the big things and the little things that matter most in their lives.

Years ago, I found myself trying to umpire a sizable conflict that had developed between a fifteen-year-old girl and her father. He had suddenly awakened to the fact that he had the makings of a beautiful young woman on his hands. Just one problem: He didn't like her taste in clothes, music, or girlfriends, and he figured it was just a matter of time before the guys would be calling. As he asserted more of his will into her life, she wanted nothing to do with it. The sticky point for her was that she felt she hadn't mattered much to him as she was growing up. Her interests weren't his interests; her concerns weren't his concerns. Suddenly, his desire to get more involved in the details of her life caused her to look at him as an unwelcome intruder. An interesting exchange of words in my office one day exposed the bigger problem. In the process of arguing in front of me, I saw why this father was having such a difficult time connecting with his daughter. The argument went something like this:

Daughter: Do you remember last summer when you came to the church to pick me up from camp?

Dad: Yeah, what about it?

Daughter: Do you recall the conflict we had?

Dad: No, what conflict?

Daughter: About Sasha!

Dad: Oh, that?! You bet I remember *that*, all right. You were so disrespectful to me. [At this point the father turned to me to fill in the details—that he had waited in the church parking lot for about an hour, the buses were late, and when she finally arrived, it was complete pandemonium—hundreds of kids, hundreds of parents.]

Me: So what about Sasha?

Dad: Well, I located my daughter, gathered up her stuff, and I'm carrying her luggage and sleeping bag to the car . . .

Daughter: [Interrupting] And telling me how much you were in a hurry the whole time we were heading for the car.

Dad: Anyway, she suddenly says something like, "Oh, Sasha! I can't forget Sasha," and goes running back to the group. So I'm waiting at the car for about five minutes, and she's still racing around though the crowd looking for this Sasha girl. I go over to her, and she's got this panicked look on her face. So I went up to a couple of the youth leaders and asked if they'd seen a girl named Sasha. They gave me these blank looks and offered no help. After a while, the group had thinned out. A lot of the parents had left with their kids. I figured that Sasha's parents must have come and picked her up or that she'd gotten a ride with someone else.

Daughter: And that's when you demanded that we get in the car and go home.

Dad: Yes, that's right! We had been there long enough. You hadn't found this girl among the people, and you hadn't found her when you went all the way into the youth offices. You even tried chasing the buses down as they were leaving the back parking lot, as though they would take off with kids still on board! You were acting like a crazy person. I didn't have all day! [He looked back to me.] So she didn't say a word the whole way home and moped around the house all evening. I figured, *A lot of good that camp did.*

Daughter: So, Dad, you wonder why I don't want you rooting around in my life?

He seemed taken aback by this question that came out of left field.

Daughter: Sasha's a good example. You don't even know who she is.

Dad: How am I supposed to know the names of all your friends?

Daughter: That's just it, Dad, you *should* know the name of this one. Sasha isn't a girl. She's a *doll*! She's the doll that I've slept with every night since I was a baby. I carried her around the house all through childhood. I've probably said her name a thousand times within earshot of you. I had taken her to camp so she could keep me company at night just like she's done since I was little. I'd put her under the strap that was around my sleeping bag, but somehow, she'd slipped out. I had lost her, Dad, and was desperately trying to find her, but you had no clue who she was and why I was in such a panic. All you cared about was getting home. If I were important to you, then you would care about the things that are important to me.

Me: Did you check the lost and found? Did Sasha eventually show up?

Daughter: No. I haven't seen her since I got off the bus from camp.

It's hard to build a significant purpose into people we aren't paying careful attention to. It's our attention to the finer details that tells them how much they truly matter to us. Our gracious God is a God of details. He knows how many hairs are on our heads.[9] He's interested in us because we are fascinating to Him. Children who get the same treatment from their parents—the same treatment that their parents get from God—grow up feeling significant. A deep sense of significance makes it a lot easier for them to find their purpose and to live it out.

3. Children feel significant when they are gracefully admonished.

Rules.

Moral guidelines.

Consequences.

All these are standard ingredients of grace-based homes. Kids with clear and responsible leadership in their lives are less susceptible to the call of the wild. Obviously, they are born with a bent toward selfishness, and they will no doubt want to put your moral boundaries to the test. But the lure of sin loses a lot of its potency when a life of grace is so attractively modeled around them every day.

Obviously, they will succumb in small ways and large ways. When they do, they need our response rather than our reaction. Sin represents a clear and present danger to our children as they try to achieve a significant purpose. That's why we need due diligence in guarding their hearts for them when they are young and teaching them how to guard their own hearts as they get older. Guarding a heart isn't a difficult skill for them to master if they are used to seeing it modeled by you. And when they fall short, discipline and consequences—gracefully applied—communicate the incredible worth you place on them.

Listen to how the writer of Hebrews makes this point:

It is for discipline that you endure; God deals with you as with sons; for what son is there whom his father does not discipline? . . . Furthermore, we had earthly fathers to discipline us, and we respected them; shall we not much rather be subject to the Father of spirits, and live? . . . All discipline for the moment seems not to be joyful, but sorrowful; yet to those who have been trained by it, afterwards it yields the peaceful fruit of righteousness. (12:7, 9, 11 NASB)

"Yet to those who have been *trained* by it . . ." Did you catch that? *Trained* by it. Discipline is one of the key tools God has given to help us groom our children for greatness. To avoid disciplining your child because it makes you feel uncomfortable is to say you love your own best interests more than theirs. Grace-based parents want to see the "peaceful fruit of righteousness" growing in their adult children. The time to plant the seed is now, and one of the ways is with consistent and graceful admonition.

MORE IMPORTANT THAN YOU THINK

A lot of parents are convinced that their kids could care less about them. Maybe it's because we've squandered too many opportunities to show how much they matter to us. We've been too busy when they needed our attention, we've been too harsh when they've let us down, and we've been too skeptical when they let us peek at their dreams. They long to have a significant purpose, and they long to know that their purpose matters to us. It's not too late.

It's never too late.

John Hickam found that out. In spite of the ridicule he threw at his son, and the reluctant manner in which he offered Homer help in pursuing his interest in rockets—when it came down to the bottom line, he meant everything to his boy. John's eyes were opened to the significant place he held in his son's heart through an interchange he had with him shortly after he arrived home from St. Louis after winning first place in a national science contest.

Homer had not realized that his idol, Wernher von Braun, had actually been at the St. Louis Science Fair. After Homer was awarded the first prize, there was an explosion of adulation directed at him. People crowded around to shake his hand. One of those hands belonged to Wernher von Braun, but he didn't know it until someone pointed to Dr. von Braun disappearing through the crowd. Homer's father couldn't help mentioning this lost opportunity to his son. Listen to this exchange.

John Hickam: I hear you met your big hero . . . and didn't even know it.

Homer Hickam: Look, I know you and me don't exactly see eye to eye on certain things. I mean, we don't see eye to eye on just about anything. But Daddy, I've come to believe that I've got it in me to be somebody in this world. And it's not because I'm so different from you either. It's cause I'm the same. I can be just as hardheaded and just as tough. I only hope I can be as good a man as you are. I mean, sure, Dr. von Braun is a great scientist. But he isn't my hero.[10]

And as Homer Hickam looked deeply into his father's eyes, his dad finally got it—*he* was Homer's hero whether he deserved to be or not.

It's almost mystifying, but it's true. We matter more to our kids than we realize. They were born

> And as Homer Hickam looked deeply into his father's eyes, his dad finally got it—he was Homer's hero whether he deserved to be or not.

with a need to make a difference. For good or for ill, we play the biggest role in determining what kind of a difference they will ultimately make.

And we know that in all things God works for the good of those who love him, who have been called according to his purpose. (Romans 8:28)

CHAPTER 5

a Strong
Hope

As I drove up to the school, I was thinking about the last time I had been summoned to a principal's office. It had been more than three and a half decades earlier. On that occasion, I didn't have to drive. I simply walked down a few flights of stairs and through a couple of hallways. My civics teacher had been in the middle of a lecture when a messenger from the main office arrived with a note. Glancing it over, he looked across the room at me and then announced to the entire class, "For some reason, the principal would like to see Mr. Kimmel."

I was not in trouble this time. In a very serious manner, the principal informed me that Dr. Martin Luther King Jr. had just been shot in Memphis. About a third of our student body was black, and the principal said he had made the executive decision to send everyone home early. He would use the intercom to make a schoolwide announcement, he said, and then turn the microphone over to me. He wanted a member of the student body to lead the school in prayer for Dr. King's family and for the nation.

When the principal mentioned the second part of his plan, I figured he had me confused with someone else. My faith was new, and my spiritual gifts were underdeveloped. I tried to explain this to him, but he simply wasn't in the mood to discuss my concerns.

It was a dark day when the cloud of hopelessness that had been hovering over our nation seemed to drop to street level—causing the entire country to grope around in its murkiness for meaning. What a time of turmoil—the assassination of President Kennedy, the antiwar protests and the "make love, not war" slogans, and now an icon of the civil rights movement had been murdered. A voice that had represented hope for a significant percentage of our population had been silenced. Like a period before the end of a sentence, people were left wondering what was and what might have been. The riots, the looting, the burning, and the curfews that followed formed the logical backdrop for that era of despair.

Déjà vu all over again

And here I was, thirty-five years later, making my way to a principal's office again. This time I would gather around a large boardroom table with area pastors, rabbis, priests, and counselors to get a grasp on the sense of hopelessness that had fallen over one of our local junior high schools—the one that my youngest son was attending. Two days earlier, one of the students had hanged herself. When she had done this, the dirt was still fresh on the grave of a fellow student who had hanged herself a couple of weeks before. Adding to the pain was the fact that less than a year earlier, a seventh-grade boy from this

When three junior high students take their lives within a ten-month time frame, it gets everyone's attention.

94

same school had shot himself. He had done it in his backyard, right in front of his mother.

When three junior high students take their lives within a ten-month time frame, it gets everyone's attention. The religious leaders of our community were gathering to be briefed by the principal, to get some questions answered, and then to try to figure out how we could help. Obviously, I believed that some of the religious leaders assembled in that room had better answers to the question than others, but there was one thing on which everyone seemed to agree: Without hope, it was next to impossible to keep a child from self-destructing.

IT'S FUNDAMENTAL

Anything—minus *hope*—equals nothing. Hope is the human equivalent of oxygen when it comes to a person's ability to live effectively. Take it away, and everything else becomes irrelevant. Without hope it is impossible to live a *balanced* life. Far worse, without hope, people surrender too soon and die too young.

The plague of today's children is a foreboding sense of hopelessness. It is the logical consequence of a generation of parents who took the permanence out of love and the absolutes out of truth. Premarital sex, cohabitation, divorce, and a series of live-in lovers have communicated to too many children that they can't put any hope in commitment. Whether we're operating in the physical, emotional, intellectual, or spiritual dimensions of our lives, hope determines our bottom line. Of the three driving inner needs, the first two rest upon strong hope.

A simple scenario illustrates this point. Let's imagine, for instance, that a person has found himself in a situation where the people surrounding him have extended no love, no kindness, and no grace. Because of how these people have treated him, he has found it fairly difficult to love them in return. However, let's say that this person has had a strong foundation of hope built into his core. The reality is that his strong hope can sustain him through the loneliness and frustration that accompany a loveless arrangement.

The same goes for his need for a purpose in his life. If someone was to find himself in a situation where he felt he wasn't making any real difference in the bigger picture—that all of his training and his giftedness wasn't working, he could get disillusioned quickly. But if he had a strong hope imbedded in his heart, *that* hope could help him through years of indecisiveness or lack of impact. Take hope out of this mix and these circumstances would get the best of him—quickly. A good example of this would be missionaries living in a dangerous part of the world that is hostile to their message. Without hope in the God who sent them there, the missionaries would be quick to return home, where they feel more significant.

The flip side of the scenario is equally true. Even if we are deeply loved and extremely confident in our purpose, it's easy to want to cash in our chips when hope is gone. That became painfully evident in the postanalysis of the three children who committed suicide at my son's junior high. Their families and friends loved them; they were accomplishing goals in school, in sports, and in their social lives. What they were missing was the one ingredient that made all the love and purpose make sense.

GRACE-BASED PARENTS, HOPE-FILLED KIDS

Any parent who wants to raise his or her children into strong, confident, and resilient adults has got to grasp the reality of children's fundamental need for a strong hope. Understanding this truth is not enough, though. Grace is the key because grace is a by-product of hope, and hope is a by-product of grace. Let's remind ourselves of what grace is. In simple terms, grace is receiving something we don't deserve but desperately need. When our children receive something they know is given at a high cost, it bolsters their confidence that there are things in life worth hoping for. Kids groomed in a grace-based environment find it easier to be visionaries, to trust in a better future, and to long for a greater good.

Ultimately, we want our children to place their hope in the only true God. We have a far greater chance of seeing that happen if two things occur first. One, they need to watch *parents* who place their full confidence in the only true God, Jesus Christ. When we say that we're deriving our hope from Christ, but they see a lack of joy, a lot of fear, and a lack of patience and kindness toward those who don't know Christ, we send out a mixed message that contradicts the gospel we hope they'll embrace. The second thing our children need is to be raised by parents who treat them the way Christ treats us as parents. As we've already said, the primary way Christ deals with us is through His infinite grace. Grace-based parents have an uncanny way of producing children with strong hope.

> The second thing our children need is to be raised by parents who treat them the way Christ treats us as parents.

The process of raising children in a grace-based environment lends itself perfectly to transferring this confident hope into the deepest recesses of their being. It teaches children that there are some things in their lives they can trust and depend on. Unfortunately, parental negligence—whether intentional or unwitting—can set a child up to struggle with hopelessness and feelings of inadequacy for a *lifetime*.

That last sentence comes across like a dog suddenly baring its teeth. The beginning of this chapter talked about the hopelessness surrounding the death of Dr. Martin Luther King Jr., the three suicides at my son's junior high, and the fundamental role that hope plays in a child's ability to love and to have a purpose. And then, *grrr* . . . you read that *you* could be responsible for messing up your children's entire lives—maybe even helping them self-destruct, simply because of your lack of awareness of the role of hope. It's unfortunate, but true. Since most people would rather feel good than do good, this is where a lot of folks might prefer to snap this book shut. That's always your prerogative, but I hope you'll stay tuned. Parents who figure out how to move hope from a fundamental need in their own lives to one of the anchor tenets of their soul become better, more contented people, and far more effective parents—period.

innate helplessness

One of the first things we need to understand is the role that helplessness plays in building a strong hope into our children. Their early ability to trust us in the areas where they are helpless to meet their personal needs weighs heavily in their ability to ultimately trust God as they grow older.

Children are completely helpless when they're born. If you strap a four-month-old child in a highchair and leave him there, there is absolutely *nothing* he can do to get out of it. He is stuck there until you lift him out. An infant left on his own for long periods of time this way is taught that no matter how much he hopes for relief, no relief is coming. If there are enough scenarios like this in his early life, he could assume that there isn't much in life worth putting his hope in. This makes him vulnerable to embracing Satan's counterfeits of power, control, or abuse as substitutes for hope, and conditions him away from the notion that it is even worth it to put his trust in God. If he can't trust the adults in his life when he is helpless, why should he assume that he could trust in a God he can't see—especially if that *trust* in God is preached to him by the parents who failed to help him in his time of need?

> Children develop hope when they have loving parents ready to sacrifice to meet their helpless needs.

I'm convinced that we unwittingly set our children up for a lifetime of struggling to hope and trust in the Lord by putting them in an understaffed, overworked childcare environment for the first few years of their lives. When their helpless needs go unmet for long stretches of time, eventually the children come to the conclusion that this is just the way life is: hopeless.

Children develop hope when they have loving parents ready to *sacrifice* to meet their helpless needs. Newborns can't feed themselves, burp themselves, change themselves, or move themselves. They can't walk or talk or read. They can't get up and check things that go bump in the night. They are completely dependent on the people around them for their existence. It's during this stage that parents can lay a solid foundation for a strong hope. At every stage of childhood—toddler, young child, elementary school child, junior higher, and even high schooler—there are built-in dilemmas that children have little to no power to deal with. They need a mother or father who has an eye on them and a savvy sense of timing that pulls up next to them with what they need to get them through. It's not that they need a handout as much as a hand up when they are facing something too big to handle by themselves.

In the animal kingdom, most animals reach a mature level of self-sufficiency very quickly. Not so with God's highest created beings. He made them helpless and keeps them that way not only to show them their driving inner need for strength and sufficiency, but also to give us as parents a perfect staging area to instill in our children a strong and sure hope in God. Take their helplessness when it comes to their need for food, clothing, and shelter. How we come alongside to make sure they are adequately clothed, have a safe and comfortable bed to sleep in every night, and never have to concern themselves with where their next meal is coming from gives them a calm assurance that there is someone looking out for them. They don't have to wonder, they don't have to worry, and they don't have to fear.

We instill a strong hope in our children when we curb our own wants in order to guarantee their needs. By living below our means and avoiding the tyranny of excessive consumer debt, we free ourselves to provide for these physical needs and keep our children from having to sense the helplessness of financial bondage.

Infants, as I mentioned earlier, are completely helpless. We can condition them to trust in the God of hope by creating a balanced and grace-based environment that accommodates their helplessness when it comes

One area that desperately needs a touch of grace is the whole issue of schedule feeding.

to their need for food. Regarding this, one area that desperately needs a touch of grace is the whole issue of schedule feeding.

Most children *naturally* fall into a predictable schedule for eating. A mom and dad can get fairly adept at predicting when the child will need to eat. It's also true that careful attention to his natural food demands can help a mother know how to satisfy her child in the afternoon and evening feedings in such a way that the child is more inclined to sleep through the night. There's nothing wrong with that. Mostly, it's common sense.

But I've noticed a *strident* attitude that is too often brought to the issue of a child's feeding schedule. Usually its advocates tout the tremendous benefits this strict view of schedule feeding brings to the *parent*—especially in the area of sleep. But without a clear commitment to grace, strict and nonnegotiable attitudes toward schedule feeding can do far more long-term harm than good. At its worst, this attitude can cause dehydration and malnutrition problems in the child. But even short of that, it can also unwittingly work to undermine a child's ability to trust his parents to accommodate his helplessness. This can cause the foundation of hope that they are building under their child to be flawed and weak.

To fall short of the stricter, strident form of schedule feeding that these outspoken advocates teach is to be guilty of feeding on demand or caving in to a child's unnecessary whims. Guilt or fear of making a mistake can keep some parents from meeting a child's genuine hunger need as well as undermine their capacity to develop a strong and supernatural hope in their hearts. Unfortunately, serious problems can develop when parents take what these advocates teach and apply their advice to their children in strident, uncompromising ways.

Personally, I lean more toward the camp of parents who orchestrate a reasonable feeding schedule for their babies. Usually everyone in the family circle, including the baby, tends to function better with the structure that accompanies this method of feeding. It is to be preferred to the philosophies of feeding that lead to overattachment, overdependence and overprotection, but there needs to be a commitment to grace that permeates this plan.

Grace doesn't fit well with stricter models of parenting. Grace often contradicts parenting plans that want to distill roles down into checklists. Grace-based parenting is a heart-activated plan that takes its cues from a daily walk with Jesus Christ. Because of this, grace and strict parenting textbooks will never find themselves in agreement.

LeT's Dance

Raising children isn't a march with a distinct left-right-left-right cadence. It's a flowing dance where the rhythms change all the time. Many factors can alter the child-raising rhythm, such as:

→ the stages children go through

→ the cycles that the parents' marriage is going through

→ relocation

→ changing economic options

→ individual setbacks

When we insist on distilling our roles in our children's lives down to a predictable cadence—especially in areas where they are helpless—we may live in quieter homes and sleep sounder at night, but we may miss the greater opportunity to equip a child with a large capacity to hope and trust. Parenting hopeful children isn't convenient, just kind. If we fail to respond graciously to the changing rhythms—both immediate and long-term—our children could wonder if we even have a clue as to what they are up against. When it comes to raising kids, grace-based parents tend to dance better than they march.

I HATE TO BE A NAME-DROPPER, BUT JESUS SAID . . .

Jesus gives us a clear example of how we are to deal with our children's helplessness by how He dealt with the helplessness of the people He encountered. For instance, everyone is born with both a physical and a spiritual hunger and thirst. As the Lord parents us, He loves to meet our powerful spiritual needs with His grace. His grace is timely and extremely generous. Listen to how Jesus summarized this:

> I am the bread of life. He who comes to me will *never* go hungry, and he who believes in me will *never* be thirsty. (John 6:35, emphasis mine)

When Jesus encountered a helpless woman from Samaria—a woman shackled by years of sin and hopeless to solve her own problem, He said to her:

> If you knew the gift of God and who it is that asks you for a drink, you would have asked him and he would have given you living water. (John 4:10)

When Jesus fed five thousand people with a kid's Happy Meal, you see His generosity and balance:

> Jesus then took the loaves, gave thanks, and distributed to those who were seated *as much as they wanted*. He did *the same* with the fish. When they had all had *enough to eat*, he said to his disciples, "Gather the pieces that are left over. *Let nothing be wasted*." (John 6:11–12)

God comes alongside us *when* we need it, not just when it fits best into His schedule. How we respond to our children's needs—especially when they are helpless to do anything to meet those needs—gives them a living example of what God wants to offer them in a much larger realm of their lives.

In Matthew chapter 6, Jesus is finishing up teaching His famous Sermon on the Mount. It's a message where He didn't lean on clever alliterated points and touching poems. From the first words that passed His divine lips, it was obvious that He didn't have any fluff on His mind. Verses 25 through 34 are where He focuses His attention on His listeners' fears.

Listen, they were an anxious people. They were worried about things like food and clothing. It wasn't that they didn't have food or clothes, but in those days, those things could easily disappear on them. Because they lived in an agrarian economy, they knew they couldn't control their ability to provide food for their daily sustenance. Famines, blights, killer storms, and invading marauders could cause food lines to appear overnight. Cloth wasn't in abundance, nor were clothes cheap. Shifts in the economy could leave them with clothes too warm for the summer or too thin for the winter.

Jesus addressed the areas of their helplessness with hope. First, He reminded them that the animal and plant kingdoms were a lot more helpless than they were, and yet He lavishly provided for their needs (verses 26–30). Second, He drew a distinction between them (people who should know better than to worry about things that God has under control) and pagans (people who were clueless). Since they had a gracious God for a Father—a God who realized they needed food and clothing—they should stop worrying (verses 31–32).

Finally, Jesus gives them some more good advice. He says, "Seek first his kingdom and his righteousness, and all these things will be given to you as well" (verse 33). It's a great example for us as parents. Just as God wants to be there to meet the helpless needs of His children, we need to be there to meet the helpless needs of our children. In the process, they gain strength and learn there is hope.

Children face crises in their emotional life where they simply don't know what to do. They need us close by, paying attention to the situation and giving them the kind of help that gets them through their dilemma in such a way that they are stronger on the other side of it.

Children are also helpless when it comes to their spiritual life. They have no idea how to find the way, know the truth, or gain the life. Leaving them to grope on their own in this critical area of their lives is equivalent to handing them over to Satan personally—on a platter. Passivity when it comes to their spiritual life signs their death warrant in advance. Few find their way through to God on their own. They need loving parents enthusiastically *leading* the way.

Sometimes it's just that little bit of help that makes all the difference. You may have a child who could use some special attention in a particular area of his academic life; or maybe he needs you to show him what to do when he knows he is outgunned or overwhelmed by his surroundings; or he needs some financial help to pursue his dream of a college education. There are strident voices that advocate leaving kids in these situations to work out their problems on their own. These are outspoken voices that speak with a lot of bravado and back up what they say with personal illustrations of success—but they lack the greater dimension of grace.

You can hear stories of how children overcame their inadequacies in math on their own, stood up to the bully and ultimately beat the tar out of him, and paid for every dollar of their college education by themselves. But for every one who did, there is a far greater majority who simply gave up. They gave up and stopped trying to master a particular discipline in school, or found themselves on the receiving end of a bully's thrashing, or never came close to their marketplace potential because of their lack of advanced education. The parents who could have helped instead taught them hopelessness. Grace could have come alongside with a math tutor, some lessons in either diplomacy or boxing, and some money for tuition that might have made all the difference in the world. But more important, grace in those situations could have bolstered the children's confidence that there are people bigger than their problems whom they could depend on for help. All they needed was to have parents help them through their helplessness the way God helps us.

THEY DON'T STAY HELPLESS FOREVER

Fortunately, children don't stay helpless forever, and eventually they become old enough to feed themselves, groom themselves, communicate clearly, and even stand up for themselves. Their minds develop well enough to think inductively and deductively.

Our mistake is when we fail to relinquish our control over these areas once children have gotten to where they can handle them on their own. Parents who run their children's lives and make most of their decisions discourage them from individual thinking. This can damage their ability to learn to lean on God. It also confuses their ultimate choice to put their hope in God and could mislead them into thinking that God likes to keep them helpless, too.

That's not how our graceful heavenly Father parents us. He wants us to grow up and take on responsibility for our choices and our actions. He wants us to move to a point where we put a lot of our areas of helplessness behind us. Listen to how He put it in His Word:

> Until we all reach unity in the faith and in the knowledge of the Son of God and become mature, attaining to the whole measure of the fullness of Christ. Then we will no longer be infants, tossed back and forth by the waves, and blown here and there by every wind of teaching and by the cunning and craftiness of men in their deceitful scheming. Instead, speaking the truth in love, we will in all things grow up into him who is the Head, that is, Christ. (Ephesians 4:13–15)

God longs to see us grow in our relationship with Him so that false doctrine and clever deceptions can't get a glove on us. Obviously, He could figure out how to isolate us from these kinds of traps forever. But He'd rather get us to the point where our maturity and completeness in Him are sufficient for us to function in a world filled with false doctrine and deceitfulness—but not be the least bit influenced by it. This is a sufficiency that comes from the hope we've placed in God along the way—it's good hope taken to its logical conclusions.

Take the message we find in the book of Hebrews, for instance. The writer laments that people who should have grown up in certain areas haven't done so:

> We have much to say about this, but it is hard to explain because you are slow to learn. In fact, though by this time you ought to be teachers, you need someone to teach you the elementary truths of God's word all over again. You need milk, not solid food! Anyone who lives on milk, being still an infant, is not acquainted with the teaching about righteousness. But solid food is for the mature, who by constant use have trained themselves to distinguish good from evil. (Hebrews 5:11–14)

It saddens God that people who should be making adult choices are still eating baby formula. He wants them to be adults.

What if parents continued to feed their children baby food and Similac all the way through their teenage years? What if they forced them to sleep in baby cribs up to the day they left for college? What could be sadder? What could be more hopeless for the child? Yet that is exactly what some parents lacking grace do with their children. They keep them helpless, dependent, and vulnerable long after they are old enough and mature enough to handle these areas of their lives themselves.

It's unloving to keep our children weak or helpless. In fact, strength (and the sufficiency that comes with it) is one of the natural conclusions of love. First Corinthians 13 summarizes

> It's unloving to keep our children weak or helpless. In fact, strength (and the sufficiency that comes with it) is one of the natural conclusions of love.

this point well. Paul closes out this famous and poetic discourse on love with these words:

> When I was a child, I talked like a child, I thought like a child, I reasoned like a child. When I became a man, I put childish ways behind me. (1 Corinthians 13:11)

Childhood is a time when we should move our children from a position of dependence on us to a position of independence from us and toward dependence on God. When they are young, we *protect* them (since they are helpless), but as they grow older, we move from protecting them to *preparing* them. One of the ways we prepare them is to give them more options to make choices in their lives. When we do this, we've got to assume that they will make some bad choices. Because some bad choices will be made, some parents don't want to give them any freedom to do their own thinking.

That is a mistake. Eventually they've got to stand on their own two feet. God gives us their childhood (especially their teenage years) to let them practice making decisions under our roofs. Simple logic would say that if children are going to struggle and make bad choices, it's better that they do so while they remain involved with loving parents to help them through it. When parents don't let them practice, children often overreact to the freedom when they go to college or go out on their own. Unfortunately, those mistakes can do greater harm to them (and to others). Grace-based parenting is shrewd about helping children grow up and develop independence *before* they are sent out on their own.

Children must understand that they will run into some challenges bigger than their ability to handle them. That's where they need to be encouraged by our example to put their hope in God. They need to see us turning to God with confidence when we are afraid, out of energy, out of ideas, or out of money. They need to see how we have trusted Him to overcome our helplessness in every situation.

Remember: When they were young, they learned hope by trusting in us—instruments of God's grace—for the big things and the little things of their lives. They can learn an even greater hope as they grow up by watching *us* trust in God for the big things and the little things in *our* lives. When they encounter the issues that even we, their parents, can't help them through, our example makes it a lot easier for them to put their hope in the Lord.

WHEN WE DON'T GET WHAT WE WANT

So far, we've learned that God enables us to meet our children's fundamental need for strength by coming alongside them in their helplessness with a sacrificial and grace-based hope. Second, we learned that we further help them meet their need for strength by developing hope through the process of handing over responsibility for their lives in areas where they've outgrown their helplessness. Now, there's one more area where God wants to use us to build their hope, and that's when God chooses to solve their problems in ways that wouldn't be of their own choosing.

For instance, there are physical problems our children could have that might handicap their ability to function on an equal plane with their peers. Sometimes inadequacy hits them at the intellectual level. They find that no matter how hard they apply themselves, they struggle to rise above average. Sometimes it's a relational dilemma they can't solve. Maybe it's a coach, teacher, or boss who simply decides to write them off for no defensible reason. Or maybe it's a boyfriend or girlfriend who doesn't care for them anymore.

In these types of scenarios, they are hoping for a physical miracle, an intellectual epiphany, or a relational windfall to suddenly make everything right. The God we trust in doesn't always deal with these problems in ways we expect or hope for. Sometimes He answers our pleas with answers like "No" or "Wait" or "Later." When He does, it's because He is working to make us better and stronger and to draw us closer to Him. He has a bigger plan that this setback fits into.

Children need to have a hope in His love that enables them to trust in His character while walking down these painful corridors of their lives. For the child facing these crises, the grace that has surrounded him, the love he's been shown, and the character of the parents who gave him that grace and love provide a natural springboard for him to rest in God's final answer to his pleas. It helps him hope when everyone else would give up.

Paul learned how God sometimes gives a different response when he asked Him to take away a "thorn" in his flesh. Biblical scholars have debated what this thorn was, but for the sake of this illustration, it was something that "tormented" Paul all the time. Like a thorn that stings away at us somewhere under the surface of our skin, this problem was constant and painful. What Paul wanted was for God to remove it, but the reply he received was "No." God said to him, "My grace is sufficient for you, for my power is made perfect in weakness" (2 Corinthians 12:9).

What's great about Paul is that the hope he *already* had in God—a confidence that God is good, kind, and gracious—enabled him to accept the fact that he was going to have to learn to live with this "thorn." In fact, he turned it into a spiritual windfall. Look what he goes on to say:

> Therefore I will boast all the more gladly about my weaknesses, so that Christ's power may rest on me. That is why, for Christ's sake, I delight in weaknesses, in insults, in hardships, in persecutions, in difficulties. For when I am weak, then I am strong. (2 Corinthians 12:9b–10).

Children don't have the years of experience of Paul or the extraordinary encounters with God like he had on the road to Damascus.[1] But if they grow up with grace-based parents, the parents become a reference point that they cue off of in learning how to trust God through the pain, confusion, or rejection that surely awaits them in the future.

Paul taught this lesson as a principle for the church in Rome to follow. Here's how he put it:

> We rejoice in the hope of the glory of God. Not only so, but we also rejoice in our sufferings, because we know that suffering produces perseverance; perseverance, character; and character, hope. And *hope*

*does not disappoint u*s, because God has poured out his love into our hearts by the Holy Spirit, whom he has given us. (Romans 5:2b–5, emphasis mine)

It's almost as if Paul took his words out of the prophet Isaiah's mouth. In discussing the effect of God's tirelessness and His infinite understanding of people who have run out of answers, Isaiah says, "He gives strength to the weary and increases the power of the weak. Even youths grow tired and weary, and young men stumble and fall; but those who hope in the LORD will renew their strength. They will soar on wings like eagles; they will run and not grow weary, they will walk and not be faint" (Isaiah 40:29–31).

A CHECKLIST FOR BUILDING STRONG HOPE

With all that we've discussed so far in this chapter in the background, let's look at three things that enhance our children's ability to meet their need for hope in a supernatural way.

1. Children develop a strong hope when they know their parents recognize their God-given abilities and liabilities and turn them into assets for their future.

It's a lot easier for our children to look forward to a hopeful future if they have the confidence that we are doing all we can, while they are in our care, to groom them for the future. Probably the best verse addressing this point is one that many parents misapply when it comes to equipping their children for the future. I'm talking about Proverbs 22:6, which says: "Train up a child in the way he should go, even when he is old he will not depart from it" (NASB).

Parents assume this verse is saying that if we raise our children in a Christian home, take them to church and Sunday school, point out the pitfalls of the corrupted world around them, and maybe put them in a safe environment (Christian schools, home schools, Christian friends), then when they are older they are going to embrace the moral and spiritual presuppositions they were trained with in their youth. For good measure, parents must make sure their children memorize the Ten Commandments, attend a Christian summer camp, and that they are prayed with before they go to bed every night.

A surface application of this verse says they might be correct. The problem is, I can come up with plenty of examples of kids who were raised according to the parameters that I just outlined, but they rejected the spiritual training of their youth when they got older. When parents see this happen, they wonder if God broke His promise to them. The answer, of course, is "No." Several have written on what I'm about to explain, so there's nothing clever or earth-shattering about my observations.[2] What is more amazing to me is how so many people continue to misapply Proverbs 22:6.

The "train up a child" part has an interesting usage when you break down the Hebrew text. The expression "train up" is used in other Hebrew literature to describe a maneuver that ancient midwives used to cause newborns to begin the sucking impulse. Right after birth, they would take the juice of crushed grapes or dates and put it on their index fingers and massage the baby's gums and palate. Besides developing the sucking response, this also cleansed the newborn's mouth of amniotic fluids.

When used in Proverbs 22, the writer is saying that we should use childhood as an opportunity to build a clean and healthy thirst for life that God has uniquely designed for that child. Now, you may be wondering how I got all that out of the phrase "train up . . ." I didn't. That's what you get when you combine "train up a child . . ." with "in the way he should go." Some translations say "train him up his way," which is actually a more literal rendering of the Hebrew word *dereck*. One of the most accurate English synonyms for *dereck* would be the word *bents*. This is how this same word is translated in Psalm 11 referring to the bend of a bow.

If you were making a bow out of a tree limb, you'd first study the limb to figure out what its natural "bent" is. Then you'd string it. If you didn't do this, when you pulled the bow back, it would snap because it was strung against its natural bent rather than with it. In the same way, we are to groom our children according to their natural bents. This means coming alongside them with a plan to help leverage their *natural* and *unique* gifts and skills into highly developed assets that they can lean on in the future.

"In the way they [plural] should go" also means that we should study them enough to know which natural bents they have that push them in the wrong direction. They might struggle with an inordinate amount of fear, shyness, stubbornness, argumentativeness, dependence, independence, sexual drive, or need to take dangerous risks. We can't make these liabilities disappear, but we are to raise them in such a way that we account for them and give them tools to help process them properly.

I realize that what I just said is a mouthful. Most parents hear a laundry list like that and then say, "How on earth do I do that?" It's actually not that difficult. It starts by making sure you are developing a plan for the personal development of *your own* assets and liabilities. Your example will teach your children far more than any of your words will. The second thing you need to do is have the right attitude toward your children's bents. God made your children as one-of-a-kinds. He built great gifts into them as well as weaknesses that require them to lean heavily on Him for power and help.

We need to be enthusiastic about helping them build disciplines around their gifts and skills. This will require grace from us because our children's gifts and skills might be our areas of natural weakness. If you are a nonathletic mom, but your children see you working overtime to take them to practices and to games and tournaments, they'll see love in action. If you hate walking through art museums but your daughters see how you go out of the way to take them to a Monet exhibit, they will sense grace. These efforts give them great hope. They relax, knowing that they are being raised by parents who recognize their intrinsic worth. They gain hope when they realize that their parents aren't trying to make them into mini-clones of themselves or trying to rewire them from the schematic that God assigned to them.

We especially need grace when we address their liabilities or weaknesses. These test our patience and our sanity. Children need to see parents who approach their shortcomings without venom or condescension. As they find parents who take delight in building into them life skills that compensate for their shortcomings, they develop a strong sense of hope for the future.[3] They realize that someone in their lives loves them supremely and wants the best for them.

2. Children develop a strong hope when their parents lead them and encourage them to live a great spiritual adventure.

You may not want to hear this, but raising *safe Christian kids* is a spiritual disaster in the making. Your effort will produce shallow faith and wimpy believers. Kids raised in an environment that stresses safety are on track to be evangelical pushovers. They will tend to end up either overly critical of the world system to the point where they won't want anything to do with the *people* in the world system—an idea that comes directly from Satan's playbook. Or, they will become naive about the world system,

> You may not want to hear this, but raising safe Christian kids is a spiritual disaster in the making.

which ultimately makes them putty in Satan's hands. He chews up these kinds of people like they are spiritual McNuggets and swallows them whole. When they're finally confronted with the full thrust of the world system as young adults, few know how to turn it into an opportunity for spiritual impact.

Safe Christianity is an oxymoron, like "jumbo shrimp." Living your life sold out for Jesus Christ has never been a way to enjoy a *safe* life. It may be a way to enjoy a *good* life, but not a safe one. That's because Jesus isn't safe, but He is always good.[4] On the inside of His *goodness* (read "grace"), He offers a safe haven for a dangerous life to be lived out. That's what a grace-based home can offer, too—a safe set of parents and siblings around whom a child can make life-changing decisions such as who's going to be the master of his life.

These types of homes have families who rest in the confidence that God loves our children. The best time to begin building this kind of confidence in our children is when God gives them to us as babies. They need to spend the early years of their lives watching their parents live on the front lines of culture. But as your children get older, you need to allow them to experience spiritual dilemmas that enable them to trust in Christ and strengthen their hope in His goodness.

There *are* risks. We must put our confidence in a God who would not bring anything unpleasant into our children's lives *except* for those things that He deliberately desires to use to mold them into His image. This overriding certainty should guide us as we make decisions on how to grow our children's hope into a strong hope.[5] This is the point that the writer to the Hebrews is setting up in Hebrews 11:1: "Now faith is being sure of what we hope for and certain of what we do not see." The author goes on, two verses later, to build a case for a God who can be trusted in our day-to-day life by reminding us that this is the same God who created the entire universe out of nothing: "By faith we understand that the universe was formed at God's command, so that what is seen was not made out of what was visible" (Hebrews 11:3). What's interesting about the God of creation is that every time He made something, He commented that it was "good."[6] But notice: He never suggested that what He made was "safe." Spend a night at sea in a terrible storm and you realize just how unsafe the universe can be.

What's interesting about Hebrews 11, the famous "faith" chapter, is that it's a stroll down the biblical Hall of Fame. It lists the résumés of some of the most revered servants God ever had in His service:

And what more shall I say? I do not have time to tell about Gideon, Barak, Samson, Jephthah, David, Samuel and the prophets, who through faith conquered kingdoms, administered justice, and gained what was promised; who shut the mouths of lions, quenched the fury of the flames, and escaped the edge of the sword . . . (Hebrews 11:32–34a)

So much for safe Christianity. Continuing, the writer says:

. . . whose weakness was turned to strength; and who became powerful in battle and routed foreign armies. Women received back their dead, raised to life again. Others were tortured and refused to be released, so that they might gain a better resurrection. Some faced jeers and flogging, while still others were chained and put in prison. They were stoned; they were sawed in two; they were put to death by the sword. They went about in sheepskins and goatskins, destitute, persecuted and mistreated—the world was not worthy of them. They wandered in deserts and mountains, and in caves and holes in the ground. These were all commended for their faith, yet none of them received what had been promised. God had planned something better for us so that only together with us would they be made perfect. (Hebrews 11:34b–40)

You don't get the sense that when you sign on with Christ it helps you make an end run around the evils of the world or trials that accompany close relationships. Those who think that the wisest way to groom a child for spiritual maturity is to isolate him from the evil, corrupted world system or airbrush his childhood environment so much that it exposes only him to the good and never teaches him how to process the bad (or the counterfeit) will set a child up for a life of mediocrity at best and spiritual annihilation at worst. Just think of how ineffective our military would be if we didn't train them in simulated scenarios that reflect the *true nature* of the challenges they will ultimately meet on the battlefield. They'd be cannon fodder if we didn't create a dangerous but well-thought-through regimen that carefully brought them up to the speed necessary to survive against their enemies.

Unfortunately, when it comes to meeting our children's driving inner need for strength, it's easy to want to build a *safe* hope in them rather than a *strong* hope. That's because there are a lot of things about raising kids in today's culture that can be intimidating. We must remember, however, that there is nothing graceful or kind about letting the fears that challenge us as parents determine our agenda—especially when it comes to our children. Often, as I discuss with parents why they are raising their children in such hermetically sealed Christian environments, I hear an explanation that usually goes something like this: "My child is very vulnerable and fragile [which is true, they are], and the world is very corrupted and evil [also true], and Satan is sinister and destructive [equally true], so *therefore* we're making these choices to *protect* our child and keep him safe."

As I listen to this standard trilogy of reasons, I always think the same thing: *You've forgotten something extremely important to your child's ability to develop a strong hope and confidence in the Lord. It's true that your child is vulnerable, the world is evil, and Satan is destructive, but there is one other point that trumps all of these concerns. God is mighty! He is powerful. He had the first word ("I am the Alpha"), and He will have the last word ("and I am the Omega").*[7]

> Making safety the priority tells our children that we think God is incapable of doing what He said He would do for His children.

Making safety the priority tells our children that we think God is incapable of doing what He said He would do for His children. Obviously, God wants us to shrewdly bring our children up within a corrupted world system, careful to make sure that they don't have to process issues too big for them. Many parents assume that *all* pressures from the corrupted world are too big for their children. The fact is that without God's power working in us, no one—whether a child or an adult—is any match for the world system. But when we put our confidence in God's power rather than the safety nets we place around our children, we find that even children can learn to rely on God's overwhelming presence to protect them as well as to enable them to flourish in the world system.

Yes, I'm suggesting that Christian families would fare far better raising their children in environments where they have to take spiritual risks, but I'm not suggesting that parents raise their children recklessly. A reckless Christian family is one where children are raised in the world but are not shown how to appropriate God's power to live distinctively from the world's way of thinking. Too many parents assume that it is impossible to effectively raise kids in the midst of a corrupt world system. Obviously, they haven't given church history even a cursory look. If they had, they'd realize that we didn't get where we are today by functioning safely behind the lines of the spiritual battle.

Seeing the word *risk* and *assuming* it is "reckless" is a convenient cop-out for people living in safe, fear-based Christian circles. That's because they know full well that to effectively raise kids on the front lines of the world system would require a much more spiritually savvy parent. You can't dump your children on the front porch of the religious professionals or educators and think you've done your duty. You can't prop them up with evangelical clubs or youth programs that have them doing a lot of biblical calisthenics and think they are somehow prepared. You might actually have to lead them across the battlefield yourself. It is not an easier form of parenting—just better. In the long run, this way produces spiritually strong and sound children.

Raising children in evangelical hideaways and creating a spiritual Disneyland works directly against the development of an empowered relationship with Christ. If anything, safe Christianity isn't about a relationship with Jesus Christ; it's about a relationship with a Western, middle-class caricature of Jesus Christ. It's an option that the majority of Christian parents around the world (especially the Third World) wouldn't consider for their children because it isn't even a remote possibility. Raising safe Christian kids is as much a product of middle to upper-class wealth as it is anything else. Putting it bluntly, the reason parents choose to raise their children in highly protected spiritual enclaves is because *they can afford to*. History has shown, however, that God the Holy Spirit has always provided better protection for children than their parents' checkbooks ever could.

These protected environments don't allow a system of spiritual antibodies to develop within the character of the child. This produces a generation of people who *must stay within* a spiritually sterilized environment in order to thrive. These are nice systems that produce nice kids who marry nice kids who go to nice churches and hang out with like-minded nice friends. Meanwhile, the lost people in the world around them continue in their doomed condition. In these environments, there is little spiritual adventure. God is nice, Jesus becomes a plush toy that we cuddle, and we become irrelevant.

Wayne and Kit are friends of mine who have chosen to raise their children in the rougher parts of downtown Phoenix and have shown their children how to turn their home into a beacon of light to the hurting folks around them. After their daughter, Heather, graduated from high school, her parents sent her off to one of the leading evangelical universities in the United States—a school that prides itself in training and equipping the next generation of foreign missionaries.

Their daughter had signed up, along with some of her fellow students, to spend her spring break working in an orphanage in Haiti. The idea was to build a relational bridge with the local missionaries, and then come back the following summer for an extended time of serving the children. Everything was fine—until a phone call came into the missions department at this university. It seems that one of the mothers of a team member had read the U.S. State Department traveler's alert for people going to Haiti. Because of the unrest in that region, the State Department warned Americans heading to this fragile country that it could be dangerous.

The student's mother wanted to know if the school was aware of the State Department advisory. The missions department head told her that the school was very aware of it. In fact, he mentioned that many regions around the world that most needed the gospel consistently came up on the State Department's radar. Then the mother asked if the university was prepared to guarantee her daughter's safety. The school explained to this mother that due precautions were being taken diligently, and they had every reason to believe that the students going should have a reasonably safe mission experience. "No one can guarantee that *nothing* will happen," he said. "There are always dangers when we take the gospel to desperate parts of the globe, but we are trusting the Lord to watch over us and not bring anything our way." That was a good response—a biblical response, too.

That's when the mother stated that she would bring a lawsuit against the university if anything happened to her daughter. That set alarm bells ringing. That's when this major Christian university, an institution of higher learning that prides itself in grooming the next generation of world missionaries, decided to let their lawyers determine in whom they were putting their trust in. The attorneys, whose job it is to look out for the university's financial best interests, felt that the school would be better served if they did not allow the students to travel to a dangerous region like Haiti. Their research showed that a nearby Christian college had been successfully sued by parents whose college student was injured on a foreign missions trip. The school sided with the lawyers, the tail wagged the dog, and the missions trip was canceled.

My question would be, "If we want to build a strong hope in our children—a powerful confidence in the God of the *universe*—why don't we let Him decide where we go?" My experience has been that God is infinitely capable. That's why we have not hesitated to travel to troubled areas of the world ourselves *and* to send our children to these places, too (without us). My wife and I have worked in hot spots in Africa, Israel, and Egypt. I have been down back alleys in Indonesia, Papua New Guinea, and China. Our children have served in poverty-stricken countries throughout Central America and in Old Europe. We even allowed our son to travel by himself to India to serve there during his junior year of high school. This doesn't mean that we shouldn't do our homework and take necessary precautions, but it does mean that we show confidence that God is in control and we know what we are up against.

I'm grateful that the early disciples didn't consult their lawyers before taking their personal families and their young understudies with them to the various pagan towns that cluttered the ancient map. Had they thought "safety first," there would be no church, no redemption, no grace, and no hope.

To finish the story, Heather ended up buying her ticket back from the missions department of the school and going to Haiti *by herself*. Since the school had already arranged to take boxes of medical supplies and educational tools, they agreed to let Heather take these items along with her. This diminutive college coed flew to Port-au-Prince with full confidence in the God who sent His only Son to die for the people of Haiti. God used her in a mighty way. The trip impacted Heather like no other trip before, and because she made the spring trip, she was able to return the following summer to serve in an extended tour of missions. Heather is now married. She and her husband have an unflinching confidence in God's power in their lives.

> Another analogy of traditional and safe Christian parenting is that it's like a mighty ship, carefully built and beautifully launched, that never goes past the harbor entrance.

To many Christian parents, the idea of developing their children's faith is like teaching them to swim on the living room rug. They don't want them to learn how to swim in water because they could drown. So these children don't really learn how to live out a strong, adventurous faith; they just know how to go through the motions.

Another analogy of traditional and safe Christian parenting is that it's like a mighty ship, carefully built and beautifully launched, that never goes past the harbor entrance. The young crew studies sailing, but they never slip out into the deep water, out of sight of shore, and open up their sails.

It is tempting, for instance, to send our children to mission destinations that double as vacation spots. And when it comes to serving close to home, where's the spiritual adventure when our children go on choir tours to sing at Christian schools, youth groups, and Sunday night services at safe churches? The most dangerous places on the globe are the places that need Christ the most. That is where the adventure is lived, the hope is grown, and the strength is built. Actually, our children are often better off taking their faith to the lost and hurting people who live at "street level." These situations don't afford them the luxury of functioning on spiritual autopilot. They have to trust God in order to thrive.

The children of Israel who fled Egypt during the Exodus had to learn to put their hope in Jehovah God. Their enemies were menacing, many, and mighty. But God's people learned to trust in the Lord for victory as they watched *Him* overcome these powerful foes. By the end of the book of Joshua, however, the generation that conquered the Promised Land was starting to settle down and enjoy the fruit of their victories.

Look at what happened to their offspring. The relative peace and safety of a conquered land developed complacency, mediocrity, and indifference. The opening verses to the third chapter of the book of Judges give us powerful insight into building a strong hope into our children: "These are the nations the LORD left to test all those Israelites who had not experienced any of the wars in Canaan (he did this only to teach warfare to the descendants of the Israelites who had not had previous battle experience)" (Judges 3:1–2).

Grace-based parents don't make it their aim to raise safe kids. Instead, they want to raise *strong* kids. Spiritually safe kids seldom get to see just how wonderful and powerful their God really is. Spiritual safety is a prescription for spiritual impotency. The good news about raising strong Christian kids is that you get safe kids in the process. They know God's love, they've seen Him work, and they understand how to appropriate His power.

3. Children develop a strong hope when their parents help them turn their childhood into a series of positive accomplishments.

Our children's inner need for a strong hope has a better chance of being developed if they are surrounded by parents who have a plan to turn them into adult success stories. We need to do some basic forecasting that anticipates what our children are most likely going to need to be successful in the future and then use their childhood to put the basic ingredients in place in their life.

Our children are going to have to know how to work hard, get along with difficult people, solve confusing problems, handle money, repent, forgive, take good care of their bodies, minds, and spirits, fear God a lot, fear their fellowman very little, laugh at the right time, cry at the right time, and bring out the best in the people closest to them. This doesn't happen by accident. Our children's childhood provides ample time for us parents to build assurances into them that they have been given all they need to take on adulthood with confidence.

a GOOD exaMPLe—anD a GOOD PUSH

Grace plays a huge role in turning your children into achievers. Achievement has both a positive and a negative dimension to it. On one side, most kids are born with a lazy streak, which inclines them to aim too low when it comes to personal development. Taking the path of least resistance comes naturally.

Unfortunately, if these children want to have any hope as adults, they've got to harness their potential, discipline their desires, regiment their strengths, and face their weaknesses with courage. It's a lot easier for them to follow our lead regarding these issues than to take our advice. They need to see us disciplining our financial wants, our physical appetites, and our emotional weaknesses. When our children spend their childhood watching us grow intellectually and spiritually, it makes these goals far more a part of their second nature.

Our example is a powerful way that we can help our children

become committed to personal achievement, but it is not enough. That's because of that "lazy streak" I mentioned earlier. We've got to add to our example a daily commitment to tutoring our children on how to overcome their inclination toward underachievement. Parents who want to build any sense of hope into their children's future must learn the graceful art of "pushing carefully" by establishing realistic standards and then gently shoving them in the right direction.

It's easy for well-intentioned parents to get carried away when it comes to turning their children into achievers. Among other things, achievement can be gained at the expense of character. Cheaters sometimes win. One-dimensional people often end up with more money. Selfishness, cunning, and backstabbing are often the faster tracks to fame.

Grace dictates that we keep achievement goals in context with the children's bigger role as members of God's chosen people. They need to see their commitment to achievement as a way to glorify God as well as a way to make them more valuable to others. Grace helps us keep achievement in its rightful place, as a means to an end.

Grace also keeps us from unwittingly turning our children into overachievers. In almost every case, overachievement is at the expense of something greater than what is achieved. Whether it's sports, academics, entertainment, music, or even their spiritual lives, we've got to demonstrate grace in setting a reasonable pace, realistic goals, and willingness to acknowledge when they've had enough.

Many disciplines that parents build into their children's lives don't make them better people; they just make them more proficient than someone else. I remember reading about a father who sacrificed to educate his children at home. They became tremendous students with excellent academic résumés—and superb spellers. Soon the firstborn became a regional champion and a state finalist at spelling bees. The next child followed suit. Before long, this man's family was dominating spelling bees at the national level.

Somewhere along the road to developing a nice skill in his children's lives, this father lost sight of the bigger picture if they misspelled a word during practice. He physically abused them if they lost, and he turned achievement of a skill into a nightmare. His pride needed his children in the winner's circle—regardless of the price to them personally. Outsiders could easily see that spelling words very few people actually use doesn't necessarily make you a better person, just a better speller. His abuse became so severe that nobody was surprised when social services swooped in and removed his children from his home.

Being the best violinist in the city, the best math student in the school district, or the best quarterback in the conference doesn't necessarily make our children more valuable as people. It won't necessarily make their futures brighter either. There's nothing wrong, of course, with our children hitting these milestones if they are part of the reasonable development of their God-given gifts, but most people in the world come in second, third, or in the middle of the pack. Children need to know that their intrinsic value has nothing to do with where they place in the race of life, nor is it a statement of how much hope they really have.

Learning to Lose

The other area where we give our children hope is when we show them how to turn their defeats into accomplishments. Sometimes it's just helping them come to grips with the outcome of a score, grade, or decision that didn't go their way. Other times it is helping them with the ongoing challenges of having inherent weaknesses and inadequacies. We need to exercise patience. It's a lot easier if we focus on the long-term goal of building a strong hope. We want our children to have reasons to believe that even with their defeats, they have much to look forward to.

Sometimes their failures are symptoms of bigger problems. If children who have consistently done well in school suddenly bring home a poor report card, most likely their problems aren't academic. Their hope rises when you don't panic and you exercise the grace to deal with whatever's creating the problem. When we respond to them with an attitude that communicates, "I'm with you, and we'll get through this together," we bolster their hope. People have setbacks, people make mistakes, and people sometimes do things that are the result of their folly. This isn't the end of the world for them; it just seems like it is. Our gracious involvement in their lives will not only help them

> Their hope rises when you don't panic and you exercise the grace to deal with whatever's creating the problem.

through these tough times, but it will also help us turn their defeats into some of the best lessons they ever learn.

COOKING UP a STRONG HOPe

I've only baked two cakes in my life. Both were for my wife and both were for her birthday. The first one was when she was a teenage girl and I was trying to win her heart. The second was early in our marriage, before I realized that the professional chefs over at Safeway would make one to order and decorate it to specifications. One reason I didn't pursue my career as a birthday cake maker was because my first two attempts turned out so badly. The first was flat and the second was dry. I suppose if I put my mind to it, I could figure out through practice how to bake a fairly good cake. But it would require that I pay attention to the recipe. The list of ingredients and the amounts recommended are not suggested by accident. When you carefully follow the plan, you have a great dessert waiting at the end.

The same goes for building a strong hope into our children's lives. They need parents who *tailor* a plan to turn their unique, God-given abilities into assets, who aren't afraid to lead the way in living a great spiritual adventure, and who work to turn both their victories and their defeats into a series of accomplishments.

Abilities, adventure, and accomplishments—they form a recipe for a strong hope. And since they don't sell professionally made hope over at your nearest Safeway store, it's probably best if you learn to bake this yourself. Your first attempt might fall flat and your follow-up might leave you feeling a little dry, but you'll get good at it if you just don't give up.

> Do not be deceived: God cannot be mocked. A man reaps what he sows. The one who sows to please his sinful nature, from that nature will reap destruction; the one who sows to please the Spirit, from the Spirit will reap eternal life. Let us not become weary in doing good, for at the proper time we will reap a harvest if we do not give up. (Galatians 6:7–9)

CHAPTER 6

a Delivery System for Grace

Homegrown grace.

It's the kind you serve up in big helpings during those daylight hours when you're well-rested and in a giving mood. It's a home-baked mercy that easily oozes from families that have kids who are easy to raise.

I personally have no clue what this kind of grace looks like.

There's nothing about grace that comes naturally to me. My appreciation for this wonderful gift has grown from the myriad ways I've received it rather than the isolated cases where I've happened to exercise it.

My early years were spent being raised by a mother and father who were desperately trying to get a handle on God's grace. They went to church looking for it, but all they were shown was the grace that led to salvation. They learned about grace that would forgive them of their sins and give them their "Get Out of Hell Free" card.

Unfortunately, my parents' church left them with the impression that the grace that brought them to the foot of the cross also stopped there. Once they were inside the family of God, the focus shifted to what they owed in return.

During the church service, we sang spiritedly about the wonderful grace of Jesus. But once the pastor came up to the pulpit, we were eight Kimmels in the hands of an angry God. We never learned that God meant for His grace to also be the gentle mercy that helped us get through our shortcomings each day. No one ever explained that God wanted to reformat our hearts through His saving grace so that we could become ambassadors of this same grace to the people around us.

My family's early relationship with Jesus was less about His love for us and more about His disappointment in us. This notion, of course, led my family down the on-ramp to legalism.

In one sense, legalism is a lazy man's religion. It's an empty Sunday suit that doesn't require much of a personal relationship with God. It doesn't require much thinking either. You simply memorize the list of things that good Christians do, and then you try to check off as many as possible during the week. You also study a much longer list of things that Christians *don't* do. You have to work overtime to avoid doing these things, while at the same time avoiding anyone who does them as well.

My parents slipped into the narrow groove of legalism and found its predictability quite soothing. Our family wasn't spiritually arrogant or part of some elitist Christian faction. We were part of the middle-of-the-road group of conservative Christianity—ground zero of the evangelical movement.

Two things happened that changed it all for me. God sent a church of sleepwalking legalists in the 1960s, and He sent my family to another congregation. The turbulent sixties punched legalistic Christianity dead square in the mouth, and it wasn't a sucker punch either. Legalism not only saw it coming, it had it coming. The strident faith that emulated the Pharisees of old showed little love and offered the unbelieving world little hope. The rebellious sixties—that famous decade of Elvis Presley, the Beatles, the hippies, the women's libbers, the antiwar crowd, and the free love movement—were a wake-up call to the safe predictability of graceless faith. The popular culture rejected God as quickly as God's people rejected the popular culture.

Fortunately, God was igniting a fresh new spirit in people who weren't afraid to let His love shine through their lives. The Jesus Movement of the early 1970s fanned a new fervor among God's people. God raised up many bold churches and courageous pastors who built worship centers embodying His grace from the top down and the bottom up. But these churches were still the exception rather than the rule—especially when it came to helping parents raise effective kids. Personal behavior remained the litmus test, and that development still haunts many within the mainstream evangelical church today.

Returning to my family's story, my brothers and sister and I became teenagers during the 1960s. My parents didn't know how to handle us. The tight little formulas that distilled faith down to a list of do's and don'ts simply weren't working. Along the way, we relocated to another state and joined a nearby evangelical church. Two years later, the church brought in a freshly scrubbed seminary graduate to be its pastor. This young man came with a deep understanding of the grace of God, and he shared that message every chance he got.

This gentle giant of God's grace used his pastor's role to fill our drinking cups with living water. He fed us sandwiches made from the bread of life every time he stood behind his pulpit. He helped parents see the wisdom of listening rather than lecturing, of responding rather than reacting, of engaging rather than dismissing, of praying rather than judging. I can't say that my parents applied everything they learned, but then again we kids didn't go out of our way to make it easy for them either. When we finally tore the last month of that goofy decade off our calendar, however, we were all better off than when we started.

FRESH GRACE

Grace taught us that God cared more about the length of a child's character than He did about the length of his hair. Grace taught us that God was far more concerned about the song in a child's heart than the music coming from his stereo. I felt grace growing in my heart as I finished high school and moved into adulthood.

> Grace taught us that God cared more about the length of a child's character than He did about the length of his hair.

Looking back, I wish I could say that I parted company with legalism once and for all. Unfortunately, it was a hard concept to kill—kind of like Freddie Krueger in the *Nightmare on Elm Street* horror movies. Just when you think you've killed your tormentor, it reappears uglier and more sinister than ever. I often felt that I needed to do certain things because it would somehow cause God to appreciate me more. What a joke. How could a God who already loved me infinitely and supremely possibly love me more?

Legalism also plagued me whenever I happened to look down and get an honest glimpse of my feet of clay. Because of some of the original wiring from my early years of faith, it was hard to feel God's joy or approval, especially when I experienced fleshly encounters with my corrupted humanness. It took me a while to exhibit grace when I ran across my propensity to be prideful, stubborn, lustful, or angry. Like an old injury that acts up when the spiritual temperature changes, I found myself feeling like my relationship with God was jeopardized whenever I fell prey to the various traps that Satan sets for fools.

IT DOESN'T ALWAYS TAKE ONE TO KNOW ONE

Lest you think that being raised in strident, legalistic churches is a prerequisite to an adult life of legalism, the fact is that legalism is the path of choice for many, if not most, people who come to know Christ personally. There's something instinctive about turning a belief system into a checklist and faith into a formula. It's also easy to distill beliefs into programs and rituals that substitute for true intimacy with God. When God gives you children, you head to church to see if someone has some answers in a prepackaged and predictable plan for turning them into strong Christian kids.

If you're new to the faith, or if you've lacked decent role models, it's natural to want someone to tell you what is expected of you. It's easy to sit back and listen to a pastor dictate the way Christian parents should deal with entertainment, education, fads, and church activities rather than to embrace the "walk by faith" option that the Bible refers to. In actuality, church pastors can be powerful allies in raising great kids, as long as they don't blur the line between nonnegotiables and good suggestions. Even if they are careful not to make that mistake, many parents still choose to turn their suggestions into law. When they do, it encourages reliance on a checklist rather than on God. This parenting style frustrates children, especially when there isn't anything biblically wrong with the way they happen to be acting out their personality.

It can get downright nasty for kids in Christian homes when the plan for effective parenting is narrowed and limited in its scope. When you throw some nice guilt into the mix, legalism can appear overnight as the headmaster of your home.

matrimony and maternity benefits

Two wonderful things happened that helped grace become a staple in my personal life. First, I married a beautiful young woman who hadn't lived in the shadow of legalism when she was growing up. Darcy came from an unchurched family. It was amazing how much she taught me about enjoying the unconditional love of God. The second thing that happened was God gave us children. I had been slowly and deliberately working my way clear of the tyranny of legalism, but having children helped me make the ultimate leap into the arms of God.

One thing I knew: I didn't want my children to grow up in a home where they felt that God's pleasure was determined by their behavior. Nor did I want them to feel that there was no latitude in how they lived out the different nuances of their personalities. Strident parenting formulas have a bad habit of using spiritual molds to create look-alike, sound-alike, and act-alike Christian kids. I wasn't interested in that. It ran counter to the way God operates in His grander relationship with His creation. There's nothing about that kind of plan for parenting that encourages an original relationship with God, let alone original kids. I didn't want my children to end up as "Mini-Me's" of their parents' faith.

All that said, it didn't mean my wife and I were going to raise our children without clear moral boundaries or spiritual expectations. There's nothing graceful about a life of license. If anything, a licensed life is the shortcut people take if they really want to speed up their personal destruction. Boundaries in our life mark the demarcation between success and failure. Just like property boundaries, the lines that frame a football field, or barriers that separate us from oncoming traffic, we know that a grace-based style of parenting also requires clear boundaries for our children's physical, intellectual, emotional, and spiritual lives. We just didn't want arbitrary boundaries based on unsubstantiated Christian opinion. We wanted to rely on the boundaries the Bible clearly drew and then trust God to help us make balanced decisions when faced with the usual "stuff" that hits parents.

I realize that many will want to criticize the basic tenets of grace-based parenting because it knocks the props out from underneath the teachings that say you can raise great Christian kids by simply putting them in the right environment and programming the right information into their heads. You can't.

Because grace-based parenting doesn't magnify the minors or elevate the nonessentials, it's easy to be criticized by the people who measure a Christian family's effectiveness by how they look, how they act, how they go to church, and how they distinguish themselves from anything that strikes of the "world."

There might even be books written to counter what I'm suggesting here. I can just see the titles now—*Tim Kimmel's Reckless Grace* or *Too Much Grace: The Tim Kimmel Model*. What I'm suggesting is anything but reckless, and the last thing I want is to raise children who embrace the world's *mind-set*. Grace-based parenting doesn't assume there is some kind of external checklist that can be followed for producing solid Christian kids. Grace-based parenting works from the inside *out*. Fear-based parenting works from the outside *in*. That's why I think so many of the superficial measuring rods of fear-based parenting are so foolish—even destructive to our children's relationship with God (i.e., how many verses they've memorized, how conservatively they dress, the fact that they listen to only Christian music, etc.).

When it comes to superficial and arbitrary standards of dress and style, I'm not particularly concerned with how children look on the outside, and I don't think God is as concerned about these things as people think He is. He's more concerned with our children's hearts. I've discovered over the years that if you get their hearts in tune with God, then you can leave it up to God to figure out how they will look on the outside. If they are living a joy-filled life with Christ, and His Spirit isn't stirring them about how they look on the outside, then I don't know why we should bother them about it either. As our children grow and mature in their relationship with Christ, things they need to adjust will happen far more easily when they are prompted by God's Spirit rather than coerced by their parents.

As my wife, Darcy, and I assessed our parenting options, we wanted a style that took into account our children's unique personalities, their fragile natures, the corrupted world that surrounded them, their personal bents, and the individual pilgrimages on which God would take them. We wanted our method to be powered by our confidence in God rather than our concerns about the messed-up world we were raising our children in. And that's not to suggest we did not have concerns. We obviously did, but they were dwarfed by the infinite power of God to overcome them. The success of our parenting plan rested far more on our personal and daily relationship with Christ than any other factor. We simply wanted to make sure that our children's home reflected the spirit of the relationship that God maintains with us—grace.

GRACE-BASED PARENTING FOR DUMMIES

I have a difficult time keeping much more than three or four things straight in my head at any given time. That's why I was relieved to learn that God hasn't made this concept of parenting with grace that difficult. There are four basic things you need to do to maintain a grace-based environment for your children. If you get these four things up and running, then parenting challenges seem to find natural and reasonable solutions. These four items will become a filter system that enables you to process the day-to-day dilemmas that come with raising kids. They will help you discern how to deliver grace in any given moment. When these four things are done with the three inner needs of a secure love, a significant purpose, and a strong hope as their target, kids experience God's grace in a balanced way. This fourfold delivery system makes it a lot easier to show your children how to find love, purpose, and hope in Jesus Christ.

Grace-based families are homes where children are given:

1. The freedom to be different

2. The freedom to be vulnerable

3. The freedom to be candid

4. The freedom to make mistakes

There's nothing magical about this matrix since it's simply the sum of how God deals with us through His grace. He made us with a gnawing need for security, for significance, and for strength. He helps us meet our need for security by finding a secure love in Him. He helps us meet our need for significance by finding a significant purpose in Him. He helps us meet our need for strength by finding a strong hope in Him. The way we sense His grace each day is through the grace He grants us to be different, by the grace He extends to us when we are vulnerable, by the grace He allows us when we are candid with Him, and by the grace He pours over us when we make mistakes.

The next four chapters will take a deeper look at what this four-fold delivery system of grace looks like in grace-based families.

a matrix for grace-based parenting

FREEDOM TO

SECURE

FREEDOM TO

LOVE

FREEDOM TO BE VULNERABLE

SIGNIFICANT

PURPOSE

FREEDOM TO MAKE MISTAKES

BE DIFFERENT

STRONG

BE CANDID

HOPE

CHAPTER 7

The Freedom to
Be Different

We were on one of those family vacations that our children will never forget. France, Switzerland, and England were to be the staging areas for the Kimmel vacation of a lifetime. We had spent a week in Paris—the City of Lights—and had also ventured out to Normandy where we were sobered by the sacrifices that had been made by American GIs on its hallowed shores. We were looking forward to crossing the English Channel and enjoying the sights of London, Oxford, and Cambridge. But first, we planned a four-day loop over into Switzerland. As we boarded a train at Gare Nord, the chatter among the Kimmel kids was all about the hang gliding and mountain biking that awaited us in the Swiss Alps. Our conversations were still filled with anticipation several hours later when we pulled into the train station in Lausanne. So far, everything had gone pretty smoothly. I assumed our stay in Switzerland would be more of the same. What we didn't realize was that it would be where we encountered a major challenge to our commitment to grace-based parenting.

Upon our arrival in Lausanne, we spent a few hours checking out the Olympic headquarters and museum. That's where we rendezvoused with a wonderful lady named Ruth who owned a quaint chalet in a remote Alpine village. She was a longtime friend of Darcy's family, but was a new acquaintance to me. Ruth would be our hostess and tour guide for the next few days, and we soon learned that she was an amazing woman with an incredible intellect. Ruth could switch from French to German to Italian to Spanish to English with ease. Our children were fascinated as she seamlessly shifted between languages as if she were a linguistic automatic transmission.

I rented a Volkswagen van so that we could look more like locals than the fish-out-of-water Americans we actually were. Darcy and our two daughters got into Ruth's car while I and our two sons would follow in the van. Because I had no map, no idea where I was, and no idea where I was going, I told Ruth that I'd do my best to stay right behind her. She mentioned that we were going to be passing through several little towns on the way to her chalet and that it would be easy for us to get separated. She promised to go slowly enough for us to keep up.

Reasonable minds would have suggested that perhaps I write down Ruth's address and phone number, and perhaps ask her for a map. But that would be logical. I figured it was a day for living dangerously, and I also figured there was a much easier (and safer) way to solve the problem. So I said something like this to Ruth: "I'll do my best to follow you. If I suddenly notice that you aren't in front of me, I won't proceed to try to find you. I'll just pull over to the side of the road. Just have one of the girls look out the back for us every once in a while. Should you find that you've lost us, just double-back on the exact route you've taken, and you'll find us waiting for you."

MAGICAL MYSTERY TOUR

We had a three-hour drive ahead of us—the same amount of time Gilligan and his friends had set aside for their boating adventure. We were about forty-five minutes into our road trip when I lost Ruth in one of those little villages she mentioned that we'd pass through. Just before I lost them, I noticed that everyone in Ruth's car was deep in an animated discussion. I didn't notice anyone from my family looking back to see if we were following. Based on that, I figured it could be a while before they checked to see if we were still behind them.

I pulled the lumbering VW van to the side of the road to begin our wait. My boys and I rolled down the windows. The setting was like some of the picture books we'd studied prior to the trip: a quaint village, a quiet river flowing through the middle of town, and the mighty Swiss Alps reaching for the sky. The boys and I turned in our seats to make ourselves more comfortable. I mentioned to them that there was a good chance we might be sitting there for a while. Both boys seemed fine with the idea. Neither of them complained, or whined, or wondered. We had been taking each day of our vacation for what it had to offer, and we assumed that God had scheduled part of this day for the Kimmel boys to be sitting in a Volkswagen van along the side of a road in the middle of a picturesque Alpine village.

It was quiet until I broke the silence with what I thought was a safe question. "So, what do you want to talk about?" I asked. I realize that this question assumed that my boys would even *want* to talk, but knowing their personalities, they were content with quiet or chatter—it didn't matter to them. I thought a good conversation might make the time go a little faster and keep them from thinking about the reality of our situation, which was that we were lost, abandoned, and clueless about what would happen next. There was a long pause.

"Dad, I want to talk about bleaching my hair."

It was Cody. He was our second child and firstborn son, thirteen years old (at that time) and going into the seventh grade. Did he want to talk about if we were ever going to see Mom and his sisters again? No. He wanted to talk about his hair color. His little brother, Colt, suddenly became all eyes and ears.

Let's step back from this scene a few feet and take in a bigger picture, which was: This could be a time to exhibit grace. Back then, bleaching hair was a new thing, not like it is today. When Cody asked me about bleaching his hair, this fad was on its way in. You could count the boys in his school on one hand who had nuked their hair. It was a look that had made its debut on the heads of gangbangers (I've always been amazed at what trendsetters they are). The etymology of these fads is often why many conservative Christian parents assume that such an idea is really a *stupid* (read: horrible) idea. Why would you let your kids look like the kids from hell? What does it say about a boy who wants to identify with a style popular among people who would strip your car when you weren't looking? And the bigger question: How would this reflect on me as a parent if my church friends saw my son with his hair all goofy?

These are the kinds of questions that cross the minds of Christian parents when their children ask permission to experiment with any popular trend. These are also the very questions that prompt these same parents to tersely respond, "Sorry, fella, but no way and no how." That's because Cody was asking permission to do something that would cause people to prejudge him—and not necessarily for the good. He was also asking my permission to do something that could affect how his peer group saw him—which he figured would probably be favorable.

Once again, these are the very reasons why most parents assume the answer should be "It is absolutely out of the question." The fact that his peer group would think that bleaching his hair would be cool is often assumed to be good reason to go the other direction. Kids are immature, unreliable, fickle, and sensational—hardly the kind of foundation for determining standards.

ROOM TO BE DIFFERENT

Let's hit the pause button to make a primary point about the delivery system of grace. Grace can't be some abstract concept that you talk about in your home. It has to be a real-time action that ultimately imprints itself on your children's hearts. Therefore, grace must be quantifiable. To talk about grace, sing about grace, and have our children memorize verses about grace—but not give them specific gifts of grace—is to undermine God's work of grace in their hearts. Grace not only means that God loves them even

> Grace can't be some abstract concept that you talk about in your home.

though they are sinners, but that He loves them uniquely and specially.

The primary way to give our children grace is to offer it in place of our selfish preferences. They receive grace when we choose not to commit sins against their hearts when our human nature would suggest that it would be okay to do so. In fact, the greater grace that children receive is when we can even *see* the sins we are inclined to commit against their hearts followed by our willingness to go against our selfish urges. So much grace is stolen in the heat of a moment by our selfishness. Kids want things, need things, say things, or do things that either bother us, embarrass us, or hurt us. But sometimes the reason we are hurt is because we might be exercising immaturity, insecurity, or indifference. We take things that are huge to children and trivialize them, or we take small issues and magnify them out of proportion. Regarding Cody's request to fry his hair, I could have failed to see how important this was to him by quickly dismissing it, or I could have made it far more of an issue than it actually was.

What my wife and I have learned over the years is that grace-based homes have got to be places where children have the option to be who God uniquely designed them to be. ***Therefore, the first characteristic of grace-based homes is: They are homes that give children the freedom to be different.*** The two operative words here are *free* and *different*. It is not a grace-based home when parents allow their children to be free but then punish them for being different. If you have a different child and remind her about the sacrifice you've made to accommodate her quirks, it is not a context of grace. This happened often during the hippie movement of the 1960s. Some Christian parents let their children grow their hair long, but then they spent their time telling the world how embarrassed they were. These kids didn't feel love, pride, or grace coming from their parents. Grace-based parents gladly make room for their children's differences.

SYMBOLS OVER SUBSTANCE

Not allowing your children to do innocent but different things is the logical outgrowth of a belief system that emphasizes the symbols of faith rather than its substance. This shallow religion measures success more by the image than by genuine authenticity. It reminds me of a twist on an old saying: "It matters not whether you win or lose; it's how you look for the team picture that counts." Unfortunately, this is a gigantic and unnecessary joy stealer for the kids in these kinds of homes.

Once when I was a fairly young boy, I happened to overhear a father scolding his daughter in the church parking lot for leaving her Bible at home. In an overly loud tone, he insulted her and proceeded to inform her how disappointed he was in her leaving "God's precious Word" behind. She said she was sorry and that in a hurry to get ready for church, she had inadvertently forgotten her Bible. She promised him she'd never do it again, but then he pulled her behind the open car door and gave her a few swats on her behind. He sent her off to Sunday school in tears. Even at my young age, I knew that man had probably not spent much time reading the Book his daughter left behind.

There's more thinking like this in Christian families than most of us would like to admit. Some of it is not as hideous as this incident with the misguided father but just as sinister. When we elevate an arbitrary Christian behavior (like bringing your Bible to church) above the best interests of a child's heart, we've clearly lost our way. There's no other explanation for it.

WHAT *DIFFERENT* MEANS

Let me give you some synonyms for "different" so that you clearly understand what I'm referring to. I'm talking about "unique," "weird," "bizarre," "strange," "goofy," and "quirky." Grace-based homes should provide a safe haven for these kinds of children. Since being misunderstood is an occupational hazard for Christian writers, I need to qualify what I *don't* mean here. I'm not saying that grace-based homes should tolerate sin, or evil, or anything that goes contrary to *clearly stated precepts* in the Bible. For instance, a child who interrupts her teachers, speaks disrespectfully to people in authority, or uses caustic put-downs against her siblings can't hide behind any of the synonyms that I've listed above as a way of abdicating responsibility for her actions. She can't explain her disrespectful behavior with a throwaway excuse like, "Listen, I'm just goofy that way. Why can't you just accept me as I am?" The answer is simple: The Bible clearly states that the way she interacts with her teachers, people in authority, or her siblings is unacceptable.

But those who are just plain different and do goofy things aren't necessarily wrong. They're just *different*. Because their different looks or behavior often annoy or embarrass their parents, it is automatically assumed that whatever they are doing (or want to do) must not be tolerated. This makes it tough for kids hard-wired by God to be a bit different and limits us in being used as God's instruments of grace.

I defend the right of children to be different if for no other reason than the fact that they are *children*. They are young. Their hearts stir with an almost miraculous sense of wonder. Their young minds run wild and sometimes perform crazy gauntlets within their imaginations. God made them this way. He chose to put these characteristics on the front side of their life. Obviously, He calls on parents to help them develop the maturity and skills to take on adulthood, but not at the expense of their unique nuances. This is an amazing time of their lives. When we get done leading them through it, the sense of amazement is still supposed to be in place—only more sophisticated. Declaring war on his differences just because they don't fit our fancy is a good way to snuff out a child's sense of wonder and amazement for a lifetime.

Whenever I read great or interesting magazine articles, I file them away for future reference. I'll never forget the impact one article had on me as a father.

The writer had penned one of those "If I could do it over again . . ." type articles about being a dad. He listed various things that he wished he could go back and do differently with his children, who were now grown. One of the things he said went something like this: "If I could do it all over again, I wouldn't have made such a big deal about my son wanting to go to sleep with his desk chair on his bed." There was an explanation that went with this incredible statement. Apparently, his son (in the three- to four-year-old range) really liked the desk chair in his room. Every night, he wanted to have his mom or dad put the chair on his bed—near his feet on top of the bedspread. When they asked why, he'd say things like "I really love it" or "I just enjoy going to sleep with it." When they asked what was wrong with the chair staying where it was since it was still close by, he'd tell them how much he preferred having his desk chair on his bedspread as he fell asleep. When they resisted his requests, he'd get teary-eyed or actually start crying. His parents would then scold him, and he'd cry more. On those occasions when they accommodated his wild request, he'd always tell them how thankful he was. What was most amazing about those nights was how easily he would fall asleep.

For the most part, however, his parents (especially his father) would make a scene about putting the desk chair on his bed, which always led to the tears and the shouts. When they did let him sleep with his desk chair, they'd stop by the room before their bedtime, and invariably his sleep movements had already knocked the chair to the floor. They'd roll the chair back to his desk, wish their son sweet dreams, and close the door. Every morning, their boy was fine.

As this father looked back on those months of nights that their son had cried himself to sleep because of their refusal of his simple request, he was overwhelmed with regret. He realized after the fact that his son's request, though weird, bizarre, strange, goofy, and quirky, was not *evil*. There were no moral issues at stake, and any parent who would try to make one is simply not willing to see the obvious. This father, with the advantage of time and the wisdom gained from years of foolish decisions, wondered why he hadn't gladly picked up the chair, set it gently at his son's feet, and not made the least little issue out of it.

For the record, his son did not grow up with some kind of weird furniture fetish. He turned out to be as normal an adult as he was a boy. He just wanted something innocent that his parents chose to make an issue over. Although I laughed at the clever way this writer described his son's strange request, I resonated with his point. This was a father who wished he could go back and exhibit more grace in his son's life.

MEANWHILE, BACK IN SWITZERLAND

Which brings us back to my son. I was in a similar situation to that of the dad with a son who wanted to sleep with a desk chair. My boy was asking for my permission to do something to his hair that might cause some adults to assume that he was rebelling. You know the normal assumptions:

"He's got a problem with authority."

"He must have a chip on his shoulder."

"He's one of those shiftless kids who has no direction in his life."

These are the kinds of assumptions that adults—who should know better—often place on kids who stand out from the crowd or don't fit the conventional molds. These conclusions are seldom based on actual knowledge of the child, but rather reflect the limited scope or the utter ignorance of the adult. My son did not have a problem with authority. If anything, his request to talk about it showed the kind of respect he actually had for authority. If he didn't respect Darcy and me, he could have done what many kids do in this situation—he could have bleached his hair in private and then forced it on us. Cody wasn't a boy with any chips on his shoulder. He was a boy filled with joy, excitement, and adventure. He was a boy who was always an asset around our home. He had simply become enamored with this new fad of boys bleaching their hair.

Parents, when hit by a discussion like this, will often say to themselves, "What will my friends think?" This factor wields incredible power in how parents respond to their kids' quirkiness. Out of fear of what relatives, friends, or those in authority might say, many parents react to their children's tendencies to be different in a way that closes their spirits. When that happens, it can close their spirits for good.

Fortunately, Darcy and I have many grace-based friends. We have friends who see childhood as a time that God has set aside for children to work the "ding-dong" out of themselves. My advice to parents whose friends criticize them for having different kids: *Get new friends. It's easier than trying to get new children. Besides, you'll probably be better off.*

FADS, TRENDS, AND FASHIONS

Regarding the issue of *fads* when it comes to clothing, jewelry, music, and outside interests, should we be allowing our children to follow them? How do you raise an individual if you're always giving in to your child's desire to follow the next fad coming along? Don't kids who adopt strange looks or behaviors get caught up in the world's way of thinking? Let's take these questions one at a time.

A little lesson in marketing might help here. There are fads, and there are trends. A fad is lime-green sneakers with purple shoestrings and heels that light up every time you take a step. A trend is sneakers. A fad is a glow-in-the-dark cell phone that plays James Brown's "I Feel Good" every time someone calls. A trend is a cell phone. It's easy to overreact to what you think is a fad when in reality it's one side of a trend. Eventually, even the staunchest, most conservative parent will embrace a trend and find no problem with it.

The first thing a parent needs to do when considering a fad is check to see if there is a clear biblical precept specifically addressing it. For instance, when it comes to fashion, one of the overriding principles that the Bible promotes for both men and women is modesty. For girls and young women, that's a challenge these days. Just try shopping for something modest in any clothing mall and you realize what you're up against. Unfortunately, too many parents use this as a cop-out for loosening and lowering their standards of modesty. Besides its being lazy parenting and the antithesis of grace-based leadership, it jeopardizes our children's moral protection at a critical time in their development. Modest clothes are out there if you are willing to look a little harder and shop more shrewdly for them. If all else fails, you may have to get the sewing machine out or have your daughter wear some sort of undershirt or overshirt to cover the areas exposed by the low-cut top.

Assuming there are no biblical precepts specifically addressing the fad that they desire, there is the whole issue of the costs of the fads as well as the values you are teaching your children if you accommodate all of their desires. Let's go back to the issue of sneakers to make this point. Perhaps your son just has to have the latest shoe, the space-age ones endorsed by some NBA icon that cost $150 a pair. One of the practical ways you can handle this situation as grace-based parents is to inform your son that you're willing to help finance trends, but you don't finance fads. If he wants Shaq's or Michael's or whoever's shoes badly enough, then he'll have to earn the money to make that desire a reality. This is often the cure for kids easily susceptible to fads.

The same thing goes for music. Musical groups come and go. Some of their music is clearly antagonistic to the message of the Bible. If your children really enjoy a certain kind of sound—most likely a style of music that annoys you beyond belief—you need to *carefully* respond to their request. When children are young and far more impressionable, we need to protect them from music whose lyrics are antagonistic to the Bible's overriding message or your moral world-view. As they get older and we move into the age of preparation, the shrewd parent sits down with the children and listens to the music they're drawn to. This is a wonderful act of grace that doesn't put down their different tastes in music. Instead, this process helps them learn how to maturely process and filter the music. At times, you may have to discourage (sometimes, forbid) them from buying the CD in question.

How about the issue of raising individuals? If our children are prone to the various fads that come along, how does that encourage them to stand alone? We need to keep in mind that individuality isn't about how our children look on the outside, but rather is more about the depth of their character. Young people have always developed identities within an age group or through common goals or interests. In that grouping, there may be a tendency to adopt the group's external rituals or characteristics. That's okay. When you see a platoon of soldiers standing at attention, their uniforms and posture may look the same, but there's a different nameplate on each chest, and the same analogy works for a baseball team or a cheerleading squad. They may function as a cohesive unit, but they are still individuals.

> Overreacting to your children's desire to follow a fashion fad—especially if there is nothing morally or biblically wrong with it—could unnecessarily close you off from more meaningful relationships with them.

Overreacting to your children's desire to follow a fashion fad—especially if there is nothing morally or biblically wrong with it—could unnecessarily close you off from more meaningful relationships with them. They may figure you to be either out of touch or unwilling to hear them out. Admittedly, some of the styles that come along look foolish. Even so, grace dictates that there's room for them to be different. I think if boys started to wear knickers with silk stockings, frilly shirts with frilly cuffs, handkerchiefs hanging out of their sleeves, long wigs, and thick pasty makeup, we'd probably think they'd completely lost their minds. But that's a look that went well with the framers of the Constitution and the Founding Fathers of the United States.

Fads and fashions come and go, so it's best not to get too worked up about it. I once attended a company reception where a bunch of adults dressed in suits and dresses stood around making small talk.

One of the office underlings walked into the room with his high-school-age son accompanying him. The boy apparently hadn't gotten the memo. He wore a soccer shirt, baggy silk pants, sandals, and a three-day beard. His hair was a two-color weave about shoulder length. Yet he stood tall, looked everyone in the eye, engaged in intelligent conversation, and showed excellent manners. I knew the reason why he handled himself with such poise: his father's obvious pride in him. His dad led him around the reception, introducing his son and telling everyone about his present endeavors, and proudly explaining to his boy who the various people were and what they did. I wondered how many of the other suits and dresses climbing the corporate ladder would have been as quick to bring their different-looking kids to such a setting. Frankly, if I were the CEO, this father would be just the kind of man I'd want to bring out the best in my team.

Styles come and go. They are in constant motion. To a certain extent, this reflects the fact that we are made in the image of a God who loves variety. For the most part, fads and fashions are brief corridors the population travels through that aren't worth our condemnation. There are times in our children's lives when style means more to them than at other times. During these times, it makes sense to ask God to help you show grace and understanding.

THE OTHER QUESTION

I also hear this question posed quite often: "Aren't kids who promote these strange looks or behaviors caught up in the world's way of thinking?" This obviously needs serious consideration for those in grace-based homes, which give children the freedom to be different. We need to start with a clear understanding of worldliness and end with a clear understanding of idolatry.

Growing up, I heard the word *worldly* used from our church pulpit to describe just about anything new or different that came along. Television was worldly, movies were worldly, bikinis were worldly, convertibles were worldly, and girls driving convertibles around in their bikinis were worldly. I spent my early childhood in western Pennsylvania, Amish country. The Amish thought that things like buttons, pockets, and belt loops were worldly. If they were anything, the Amish were one of the best illustrations of the irrational and illogical nature of symbolism over substance. They were like legalists on acid. If you pinned them down and begged them to give you an explanation for their conclusions, they'd eventually quote some scriptural condemnation that they felt covered buttons, pockets, or belt loops. If you were looking for a grace-based belief system, you'd never find it in the "Amish Paradise" that surrounded us.

The standard passage of Scripture that the Amish—and some parents—turn to in order to explain to children why they can't do a particular activity, listen to a certain style of music, or dress a certain way is 1 John 2:15–17. It says:

> Do not love the world or anything in the world. If anyone loves the world, the love of the Father is not in him. For everything in the world—the cravings of sinful man, the lust of his eyes and the boasting of what he has and does—comes not from the Father but from the world. The world and its desires pass away, but the man who does the will of God lives forever.

If a noun is a person, place, or thing, and "worldly" or "world" (in this passage) is a noun, then which of those three options is it? Is it a person, a place, or a thing? The most obvious answer would be that it is a *place*. But that can't be how it is being used in this passage since we exist inside this world. If we were on another planet and looked out at planet Earth and said, "I think I'm going to go explore that *world* over there," then that usage would work. But obviously, that is not the way it is being used here. So if it isn't referring to a place, then the next assumption would be that it is a *thing*.

There are obvious uses of the word *world* where it clearly refers to a thing, but that isn't how it is being used in this passage. Otherwise, we would have to assume that we can't have an appreciation or fond affection for any "thing" that is in the world—our jobs, the places where we vacation, our church buildings, or any of the *people* in the world. That leaves one option: The world system is a person (or at least, *personal*). Thinking of the word *world* in this passage as a living organism (albeit invisible) helps us keep from misapplying this verse to the harm of our children.

The word *world* here refers to the morally evil system opposed to all that God is and holds dear. In this sense, the world is the *satanic* system opposing Christ's kingdom on this earth.[1] The "world" is a *personal* force that is operating in complete antagonism to the will of God, capable of utilizing *anything* to work its devious plans into our hearts. Because of that, we undermine our role as spiritual authorities in our children's lives when we apply the word *worldly* to specific things that we don't happen to like: strangely cut or colored hair, bellybutton rings, chopped-up cars, hard-driving music, dancing, or tattoos. What determines whether any of these things are worldly is not their *existence,* but rather *if* (or *how*) Satan chooses to utilize them for his sinister purposes in your children.

If you want to understand how the "world" shows itself, don't look at *things* or *actions* but rather at *attitudes*: the lust of the flesh (the desire for sensual pleasure), the lust of the eyes (covetousness or materialism), and the boastful pride of life (pride about our position in the world). This means that almost anything can have either a worldly or a redemptive application depending on who (or Who) we're focusing on in our hearts.

To one person, the *Venus de Milo* may be an exquisite work of art. To another person, she might be some armless hot babe from Italy, while to another person she might be some tramp that needs to wear a halter top or *something*. What's interesting about this analogy is that it is too often the Christian who attributes evil to *things* and who would be the most likely to view the *Venus de Milo* with lust. This is the logical conclusion of attributing lustful power (any power) to a carved piece of marble. In fact, it is the misapplication of evil power to things (or actions) that really allows Satan to get such an incredible stranglehold on many Christians.

When you convince your kids that *things* are evil rather than Satan and his corrupted world system being evil, you set them up to be easily manipulated by him. I knew a lady who would pick up her elementary-age children from school during the last week of October just so they wouldn't have to walk by the jack-o'-lanterns that people put out in front of their houses. She said she was frightened of what could happen to her children, but all she did was transfer her fear of jack-o'-lanterns to her children as well. They became mortified of them. This mom had attributed evil power to a carved vegetable (or is it a fruit?). When I pointed out what she was doing, she ripped into me. I got an earful about Druids (none of whom she had ever met), Satan's big party (which I thought Jesus' followers should crash), the forces of darkness (which I thought Jesus' followers should shed the Light of the World on), and all of the wicked things that could happen on October 31 (as if Satan was taking the other 364 nights off). By taking something inanimate and giving it animate evil power, she had just showed her kids how to create an idol. Their fear of the jack-o'-lanterns was giving a dead carved vegetable a power it didn't have.

God was outspoken when He commanded us not to make any graven images. He didn't scratch out His concerns on an Etch A Sketch but chiseled them onto stone tablets as a permanent reminder. Here's how He put it:

> You shall not make for yourself an idol in the form of anything in heaven above or on the earth beneath or in the waters below. You shall not bow down to them or worship them; for I, the LORD your God, am a jealous God, punishing the children for the sin of the fathers to the third and fourth generation of those who hate me, but showing love to a thousand generations of those who love me and keep my commandments. (Exodus 20:4–6)

It is idolatry to affix evil power to things or actions that are just things and actions (hairstyles, rock concerts, clothing, dancing, dating, etc.). What determines evil is how Satan is using the thing or the action in an individual's life. What determines goodness is how God is working through the thing or the action in the individual's life. What determines who is doing what is the *individual* (you, me, or the child) in the equation.

THE REST OF THE STORY

When my son broached this hair subject on the side of a mountain road in Switzerland, he was asking for his parents to see him as an individual. When he said that he wanted his mother and me to consider allowing him to bleach his hair, something very clear happened inside me. No, I didn't hear God's voice. I wish I had, but that's never happened to me. But I did sense His Spirit stirring in me—a very clear sense that God was getting me to listen to my boy's heart. So we talked. He told me why he wanted to bleach his hair (the standard, superficial reasons—his friends were bleaching their hair and it was "cool"). We talked about some of the stereotypes that people attribute to it.

As I listened, I thought of all the evidence that God was very much alive and actively working inside his heart. His attitude, his speech, his respectful treatment his parents and siblings, his love for the things of the Spirit, all pointed to a boy whose heart was in tune with God. Based on that, and the fact that what he wanted to do was something temporary that had no moral problem attached to it, I said, "Cody, I'm fine with you bleaching your hair, but I should talk to Mom about it first. If for some reason Mom is uncomfortable with this, then I'm going to vote with her, which means I'll want you to submit to our wishes without giving us any grief." He agreed.

Not long after Cody and I talked about his bleaching his hair, a frantic car flipped a U-turn and came back to find us. It was Ruth and Darcy with our two daughters. They had driven twenty minutes without ever looking back, but when they discovered that we were nowhere in sight, they turned around to hunt for us. It was great to see their worried faces, and I was glad we could continue our trip to the Alpine chalet.

When I finally got a chance to tell Darcy about the conversation I had with Cody, she said it would be fine with her. Cody was stoked to hear the news, and it just so happened that Ruth's daughter was a platinum blonde—thanks to a bottle. She had even bleached the hair of the entire men's Swiss Soccer Team. She had all the stuff to do the job that night. The whole family gathered around to watch the process and take pictures.

The next morning we parasailed off one of the local mountains. Cody launched off just a little bit before me. I could see his blond hair sticking out from under his helmet. He was waiting for me when I landed, helmet in hand, bright yellow hair shining on his head, and a grin from ear to ear. He was a fine boy, enjoying the freedom of being different in the glow of the Swiss Alps.

TWO MORE THINGS . . .

In this discussion about letting our children have the freedom to be different, two other issues come to the forefront. The first has to do with styles of fads that have a more permanent impact on our children, and the second has to do with different quirks that draw negative attention to our children.

I'm sure you've noticed how popular tattoos and piercings have become. We all know that kids have been doing goofy things for centuries. Sometimes it's to get attention from parents who aren't paying attention. Sometimes they are mirroring things they see in their parents. Sometimes there are some serious problems going on inside the young person, and these things they do are merely outward expressions or symptoms of these internal problems. Sometimes they just want to be a little different and quirky when everything is fine inside them. What do we do?

The first thing we need to do is an inventory of their three inner needs. Remember: Children have a need to be secure, to be significant, and to be strong. Our job is to help them meet those needs with love, purpose, and hope. The ultimate way to achieve this is when they find a secure love, a significant purpose, and a strong hope through an intimate and authentic relationship with Jesus Christ. This is the most important part of our role in our children's lives. When we do this effectively, the more troubling external issues are less likely to surface.

The next thing you need to do is evaluate what they want to do against what Scripture says. The Bible contains general precepts about modesty, humility, and caring more about others than about ourselves. These can give direction regarding "why" they want to do this particular thing.

> We've got to be extremely careful that we don't use the Bible to put words in God's mouth that He didn't say.

But let me point out a caution. We've got to be extremely careful that we don't use the Bible to put words in God's mouth that He didn't say. An excellent example of this is the issue of tattoos. Many people are quick to turn to Leviticus 19:28 to tell their children why they can't get a tattoo. Here's what it says:

> Do not cut your bodies for the dead or put tattoo marks on yourselves. I am the LORD.

That's pretty clear—that is, if we believe we can use a Bible verse without any regard for the context in which it appears. Many people use verses out of context to win selfish arguments and justify what they selfishly want. Using God's Word out of context to win your argument is a variation of taking God's name in vain—something strictly forbidden in the Ten Commandments. Obviously, a person that respects God's Word would desire to use it properly, especially when trying to direct a child through the maze of childhood.

If we study Leviticus 19:28 in its context, we see that it isn't talking about tattoos in general, but tattoos that identify a person with a pagan deity or pagan practice. Two verses before, it forbids the eating of meat with blood in it. Does this mean you can't eat your steaks rare? Not at all. This is talking specifically about the meat that was being offered as a sacrifice for their sin, not an evening out at Morton's. The verse directly before this verse on tattoos condemns men cutting their hair on the side or trimming their beards. Does that mean men can't get haircuts or go around clean-shaven? Of course not. In that culture, men wore their hair long and their beards untrimmed. Pagans trimmed the sides of their heads and the edges of their beards in such a way that it identified them with a specific heathen god or a specific heathen practice. That's not why men trim their hair or go clean-shaven today. When men get their hair cut, they don't light candles to some dark deity—at least not at my barbershop. They might light up a cigar, but there is nothing about that process that is in deference to a pagan deity. Therefore, this verse is not forbidding haircuts and clean-shaven faces.

Which brings us back to Leviticus 19:28. It says first that we are not to "cut our bodies for the dead." This refers to distinctive marks on the face that anyone could look at and know were part of a pagan ritual. God didn't want them giving credence to the false beliefs that attributed power or influence to the dead. In the next breath, the verse says "or put tattoo marks on yourselves. I am the LORD." Following down the contextual line, Moses is referring to distinctive tattoos that identified a person as a follower of a particular pagan deity. Moses writes that they are to make sure they don't make permanent marks on their bodies (cutting and writing) that give credence to a pagan ritual or god in a specific way.

Is this saying you can't have "Mom" tattooed on your arm? No. What it's saying is that you can't have a tattoo of your mom's name if she is also some kind of a pagan deity. Otherwise, this verse doesn't forbid the practice of tattooing. The interpretation error is in saying that this verse forbids all tattoos when in fact it's talking about specific-type tattoos to a pagan god. If your son wants to get a satanic pentagram tattooed on his arm, this verse speaks to that. If he wants to get "John 3:16" tattooed, this verse doesn't forbid it.

We need to keep in mind that tattoos are not new to the modern era. They are as old as mankind. They were everywhere in Jesus' day, just as they are today. Because of the cosmopolitan makeup of the capital city of Jerusalem, many people who encountered Jesus no doubt had tattoos. There is a possibility that the blue-collar nature of the disciples prompted a couple of them to have tattoos as well (who knows?). What is interesting is that with all those tattoos around Him, you would have thought that if they were some kind of an anathema to God, Jesus would have mentioned something about them. He remained silent on the issue. Perhaps it isn't as big a deal to Him as it is to some of us. It is man who looks on the outside, but God looks at the heart (1 Samuel 16:7).

There are two other possible references to tattoos in the Bible—at least they appear to be such. There's the "mark of the beast" in Revelation 13:16 (definitely one of the tattoos you don't want to have on you). The other possible reference to a tattoo can be found in Revelation 19:16. Jesus is described as coming back to earth riding on a white horse. He's dressed in a fine linen robe, and He has a sword in His mouth. In verse 16 it says, "On his robe and *on his thigh* he has this name written: KING OF KINGS AND LORD OF LORDS" (emphasis mine). It is not clear whether Jesus is wearing linen pants or if this majestic title is actually inscribed on His skin. We'll have to wait a while to find out exactly which way it is. But because trousers were not a standard part of clothing when the Scriptures were written—and certainly not anything that Jesus wore when He was on earth—there is a real possibility that His wonderful name is tattooed on His leg.

The reason I'm going this deeply into the tattoo issue is because it is an open-and-shut case only if you're using the Bible out of context. This is where we need to appeal to God for His grace on this matter. We need to ask Him for wisdom to help our children make wise choices.

Let me state for the record that I do not have a tattoo, my wife doesn't have one, nor do any of my kids . . . yet. I'm not writing any of this to justify my actions. The issue before us is how avoid unnecessary breaches of grace while still allowing our children the freedom to be different. Because they want to be different in ways that sometimes leave a permanent mark, we have to entreat God for wisdom.

Personally, I have discouraged—well, basically forbidden—my kids from getting tattoos. If you're wondering if Cody has raised the topic, then you'd be correct. So did one of my daughters. In each instance, I went the practical route, which *can* be backed up by the Bible. My little speech went something like this:

"I'm glad we can talk about tattoos because these days, tattoos are very popular. But they are also a fad. Because they are a fad, and because they must be painfully applied, leave a permanent mark, and can be removed only through an expensive and painful procedure, I'd rather you not get one. There is a great principle that says, 'Never sacrifice the permanent on the altar of the immediate.' What you might think is a great idea now may not look so great a couple of years—or twenty years—from now. But you'll be stuck with it. Also, a tattoo could affect some of your career options, both short term and long term. And the bigger issue is that the Bible says if you get married, your body doesn't belong to you but is the property of your spouse, as in 1 Corinthians 7:4. Since there is a strong likelihood that you will be married, you ought to wait to see if a tattoo is okay with your spouse. Regardless of any of these issues, your mother and I are assigned the financial responsibility for the upkeep of your body. Until you are completely financing yourself, we'd prefer you defer to our wishes on this. Once you are on your own, if you want to get the map of downtown Phoenix tattooed on your face, it will be completely your call."

The acceptance of these kinds of conversations is contingent on the depth of the personal relationship you have with your children. If you've been working to build their three inner needs and respond to them in grace through their childhood, the likelihood of their accepting your wishes goes way up.

As you look into your children's hearts and see no reason to question their relationship with Christ or their personal judgment regarding these more sensational issues, you have the biblical freedom to do what you think is best. If, after all your homework is done, you feel comfortable with God about it all, it looks like the Bible grants you grace to let your older teenagers and young adult children do what they want.

Some of the things that our children do to express themselves do point to some inner turmoil. But if we preoccupy ourselves with fighting them over these outward expressions, we may only make what's going on inside them much worse. We are far wiser to ignore or move past the outer problem and address the inner one straight on. Responding gracefully and deliberately to internal problems of sin, guilt, loneliness, shame, despair, anger, or fear can have a far greater effect than anything else we might do.

LIVING OUT LOUD

We've talked about specific issues children show interest in that makes them come across as different. What about the general ways children express their personalities? The fact is, many kids are just weird. Sometimes they're quirky. Sometimes they do things completely in keeping with their personality but for some reason embarrass us. How do you handle these things in a graceful way? It's actually simple. If they aren't sinning, and they are being sensitive to the people around them, you just let them live their lives out loud.

Bill and Amy approached me after I taught their Sunday school class one evening (the congregation we belong to meets on Sunday night). They wanted to inquire about their five-year-old son. Apparently, they had spent the afternoon with several other couples their age. All of them had young kids, from infants up to about six years old. In the process of gathering up the equipment from the picnic, one of the fathers had taken all the ice from the coolers and poured it into a pile in the corner of the yard. When the children saw this, they took off their shoes and started walking around on the ice. The girls were delicate about it, and the few boys at the picnic giggled as they carefully trudged around the ice cubes.

Bill and Amy's boy wasn't content to giggle and trudge around the ice. He convinced the kids to clear out of the way so that he could race across the lawn and slide face first through the ice, letting out a great squeal as he did. The kids laughed and clapped, which only baited him to do it again and again. He got his clothes all wet. He got some grass in his hair. Bill and Amy became self-conscious about his behavior. As the other parents watched, it was obvious that Bill and Amy's boy was really getting into it. His parents were concerned that their friends might think their son was out of control and reflect poorly on their parenting abilities. I'm sure some of the other parents may have felt that their son was getting carried away, but these were parents who typically feel children should be quiet, gentle, or passive.

Bill and Amy decided to intervene. Bill pulled his boy aside and told him he didn't appreciate what he was doing. He forbade the boy to slide on the ice anymore, and for punishment told him they were going to make him go to church in his wet clothes. What they wanted to know from me, as an outsider looking in, was if they should discourage their son from playing so vigorously—especially with other kids around.

"Was your son being mean to the other children or not allowing them to also play in the ice?" I asked.

"No," Bill replied.

"Was there a moral or relational issue that he was disregarding? In other words, was there anything actually wrong with what he was doing? Had you told him earlier not to do it?"

Amy took in these questions. "No, I can't say he was doing anything wrong, other than getting his clothes wet."

"Were these play clothes that are allowed to get dirty and wet?"

Both parents nodded.

"Does your son tend to play hard?"

"Yes," replied his father. "He's loud, boisterous, and is not afraid to bang his body around."

"Is he a risk taker?"

"All the time," said his mother.

"Is his personality the type that likes to make people laugh and entertain the troops?"

"Absolutely!" they both agreed.

"It didn't bother him at all that you were making him go to church in wet clothes, did it?"

"Not in the least," Bill said. "He could go to church clean, dirty, wet, dry—it would make no difference to him."

"So he was acting pretty much within his personality type, and you didn't like it because you are both much more quiet and reserved people and you felt he reflected poorly on you even though he really wasn't doing anything wrong?"

"That's correct." Bill nodded.

"So why are you concerned about what you did?"

"Because I scolded him, but I couldn't really tell him what he was doing wrong," Bill said.

"And because he cried when we scolded him," Amy offered. "I felt sorry for him. I felt we exasperated him."

"Join the club. We've all done that as parents. You've got a good boy, but he is not hard-wired like either of you. He has a loud and aggressive personality that enjoys making people laugh. Those are all wonderful qualities that, if developed over time, will be a great contribution to the future. This is where grace makes such a difference."

You might have children who are the life of the party, automatic leaders, shy, inquisitive, born doubters, soft-spoken, loud, quick to tears, stubborn, easily distracted, or very serious. Grace can be one of the best tools you use to help them live out these personality quirks in balanced ways.

PARTING WORDS

I realize how easily I can be misunderstood on this subject. Parents who want to raise kids in a safe and highly controlled environment could well think that all this stuff about making allowances for your children's benign quirks smacks of too much leniency. I'm not advocating raising out-of-control, over-the-top kids. But inside the boundaries of respect and honor, there's room for our children to be the creative individuals God made them to be. It's how Jesus parents us. I have a lot of confidence in His example.

A few weeks before our son Cody headed off to college, he and I had been sitting out on the patio chatting about different things when I mentioned to him what a handsome person he had grown up to be. What surprised me was that he brought up his hair. "What do you think of my hair color?" he asked.

I looked at his brown hair—his *natural* hair color. Sure, it had been several shades lighter a few years earlier, but for his last two years of high school, he had let his hair grow out in its natural color.

"I like it," I said. "It looks real good on you." That's when Cody said something that reminded me that grace has a tremendous payoff.

"You know, Dad, I appreciate that you didn't make a big deal about bleaching my hair in Switzerland," he said.

"That's nice of you to say, Cody."

"Yeah, I got all of that out of my system. With college on me, I figured it's time to put all of that kind of stuff behind me."

Hear, hear.

CHAPTER 8

The Freedom to Be Vulnerable

The nature of a child's spirit begs a tender touch. Sometimes it's a spirit lost in confusion and badgered by fears. Sometimes it's a broken heart that longs to recover in the deep, quilted comfort of gentle understanding. Occasionally it's a hope too good to be pursued in vain and too delicate to be pursued alone. On the front side of every life is a boy or girl in a fragile state of flux.

As adults, we know that those who follow the well-worn path to the base of the cross find ample room for heavy hearts and hurts that can't seem to heal. It's an amazing grace that doesn't trivialize the fickle nature of our personalities. There's no condescension waiting to counter our tendencies to become easily embarrassed. There are no lectures longing to straighten out the folly of our thinking. There's no mocking of our self-conscious thoughts—just a generous Savior with a gentle heart who knows how unsure we often are about ourselves.

God doesn't "card" those who come searching for His grace. You won't find any age restrictions for those wanting to travel down His path. Jesus said, "Let the little children come to me, and do not hinder them, for the kingdom of heaven belongs to such as these" (Matthew 19:14). But some paths are easier to take when they are walked hand in hand with someone older and wiser.

GATEKEEPERS OF HIS GRACE

One of the great things about God's grace is the safe haven it offers to a transparent heart. He doesn't require masks in His throne room. I know. I've been there.

Jesus makes people feel comfortable even when He catches them without their makeup. When circumstances scrub off the layers of their self-confidence, and their shortcomings wash away the foundation of their self-righteousness, Jesus isn't appalled by the blemishes He finds underneath. There's no sin too bad, no doubt too big, no question too hard, and no heart too broken for His grace to deal with.

> God has given parents the responsibility to be the gatekeepers of His grace.

These are the very things that children need to learn early on in their lives, and God has given parents the responsibility to be the gatekeepers of His grace. It is your careful response to these fragile issues that plays the key role in whether your children will even be inclined to head down the path to God's grace. Further, seeing your regular trips down this path for your *own* personal vulnerabilities makes it easier for your children to trust you when you try to take their hands and show them the way.

I remember when Claudette, a close friend of one of our daughters, was in elementary school. An early release of certain hormones caused her to "blossom" ahead of schedule. By the fifth grade, Claudette looked like she was about to graduate from high school. Here was a girl with a fifth-grade intellect, a college coed's body, and the emotional sophistication of a ten-year-old. When I got wind that her parents were followers of Jesus, I started to feel better for her. Life is vulnerable enough for a little girl without the added burden of being trapped within a mature woman's body. It's much easier when the emotions, the intellect, and the body arrive at the same *mature* intersection at the same time.

There was the obvious problem of being physically ahead of all the girls in her class. Instead of feeling like she was part of the club, she felt more like a freak show. The girls in her class viewed her either as competition or as an outsider to their peer group. Only a few treated her like she was one of them.

The boys in her class fell into a couple of categories. There were those on the cusp of puberty who made comments laced with sexual innuendo. They teased her to her face or made jokes about her that made their way back to her through the grapevine. Another category of boys in her class simply didn't know how to deal with a fifth-grade girl built like their mothers. Claudette's biggest challenge, however, was the high-school-age boys in her community. They not only noticed her, but they also saw a naiveté that could be exploited. The rejection by her peer group put her in a position to be easily used and ultimately abused by those four and five years older.

This is a time for a mother and father to exercise a keen sense of the *obvious*. Claudette was vulnerable to developing a wrong view of her peers, of the older boys that found her so interesting, and of herself. She especially needed a dad who could see that she was emotionally immature and in bad need of someone to run interference for her. She also needed to have the kind of regular affirmation from a father that keeps a girl from feeling needy for the wrong kind of attention.

Unfortunately, her parents didn't see it that way—or they just didn't see it at all. Rather than doing the math and figuring the obvious, they ignored her dilemma. It wasn't as though she didn't let them know she was struggling. She told them about the girls at school and how they distanced themselves from her. She told them about the taunting of the boys. And they could see for themselves the interest that the older boys in the neighborhood had in her. But her parents treated her as though *she* was the problem rather than the one *with* a problem.

I met her father and talked with him about some of the general challenges we all have in raising kids. It was then that I realized Claudette was on her own. Her dad was an opinionated, caustic man with little logic to back up his opinions. When I talked about spiritual things with him, it appeared he knew God, but it also appeared that he hadn't invited God to have much control over his attitudes. He spoke with bravado when he talked about how girls were supposed to act, but he didn't understand that kids often have stuff they are dealing with that makes it tougher for them to *even know* what to do. Not only are they sometimes terribly confused, but they can also get extremely frightened. This is a time for grace that notices what they are going through and comes alongside with genuine help.

Claudette's father, who told me that he had been disappointed in the choices his two older daughters made regarding boys, didn't have much confidence that Claudette would choose wisely.

I didn't either, but my reasons had nothing to do with her. She had an unusual challenge before her that called for extraordinary grace from her parents, who weren't in the "grace" mood. I wasn't surprised to hear about some of the tragic losses of dignity that Claudette suffered as she moved from girlhood to womanhood.

You can guess how her story ends. After high school, she lived with a guy for a while, got pregnant, but ended up on her own. At this writing, Claudette is twenty-three years old. Most of these years have been heartless and hopeless for her. A grace-based home could have changed all of this for her.

THE SECOND CHARACTERISTIC
OF GRACE-BASED HOMES

In the last chapter, we learned that grace-based families give children the freedom to be different. It's not a crime to be an individual in these homes. *Now let me introduce the second characteristic of grace-based homes: They are homes that give children the freedom to be vulnerable.* Children are born with an unsophisticated set of emotions. It's not that their emotions are underdeveloped. It's simply that they haven't had the time to temper them within the crucible of daily life. Their immature emotions can often prove unreliable for the situations they find themselves in. They are prone to vast mood swings, vain imaginations, and inordinate fears. They need to be in a home where parents don't overreact, underreact, or write them off.

It's easy to end up being guilty of doing any of these three things. Our children have a crush on someone, and we dismiss it by calling it "puppy love." They are afraid of new challenges posed by advanced placement classes, and we categorize it as "no big deal." They are hurt because they sense no one likes them at school, and we tell them they're probably "imagining things." We say these things not because we don't care for our children. We say them because when we step back and put their situation in the bigger context, our response might actually be correct. Our kids aren't in love as deep as they think they are, aren't in as great an academic peril as they assume they are, and may be a lot more popular than they realize they are. In other words, it *is* puppy love, it *isn't* a big deal, and they *are* imagining things. But what they need at these points of vulnerability is not some quick assessment (regardless of how accurate it is) but some gentle understanding. I say this for two reasons:

1. We need to treat our kids the way God treats us.

The Bible says, "Casting all your care upon Him, for He cares for you" (1 Peter 5:7 NKJV). It's amazing how inclusive the word *all* is. It doesn't say that we are to cast only our *legitimate* cares on Him. Frankly, I wouldn't begrudge God if He *had* said that. Although He's a busy God with a lot on His plate, He's also an omnipotent God, so He's never too busy. Nevertheless, it would seem reasonable, at least from a human perspective, not to bother God with things that stem from our children's immaturity and lack of sophistication.

Fortunately, God is a God of grace. He loves to give us things we don't necessarily deserve but desperately need. He knows we often lack perspective, but that doesn't stop Him from inviting us close to His heart.

A good example of God's grace is not only the gigantic act of grace that Jesus showed by dying on the cross for our sins, but also the little acts of grace He demonstrated in the *midst* of His crucifixion. I think most people—including the most ardent critic of Christianity—would agree that if there was any time in Jesus' earthly life when He actually had the right to be a bit self-absorbed, it would be when He was hanging on the cross. Man hasn't come up with a more horrific way to torture someone than nailing him to a cross and standing back while he endures a slow, agonizing, and lonely death. In the midst of that agony, the utter focus of pain in a human's mind would make it hard to think of anything else.

But He did. There were some people at Calvary who needed a personal touch of His grace. For most of them, they needed it because of what His crucifixion was costing them personally.

There were soldiers at Calvary who were simply following orders. They didn't realize that they were driving nails into the hands of the One who had created them. They had no idea that the man they were executing was actually taking a divine dive for them. Because they were so used to crucifying the underbelly of the criminal community, it was standard for them to show such low regard for their victims.

A fickle crowd hovered around the foot of the cross. Some came out simply to see someone being put to death. It was the Roman equivalent of a "reality" show that few wanted to miss. There were also the duped sheep—those who didn't know much, read much, or think much. They were part of the mob who would chant whatever you told them to.

Then there were the men who *wanted* Him there, who *needed* Him there, and who helped *put* Him there. These were the professional-theologians-turned-powerbrokers who had seen Jesus as bad for business around the temple. They couldn't see the crossbars that hovered above each of their heads. They couldn't see the thin strings that came from those crossbars that moved their arms, made them jump, and manipulated their mouths. They couldn't see the evil hands of Satan, using them like marionettes to do his bidding.

But Jesus could. He could see the religious leaders being used, He could see the crowd being manipulated, and He could see the soldiers doing what they were ordered to do. The fact that He even bothered to notice these things tells us so much about His grace. He did notice them, and in the process He did something to give all these people a gift they desperately needed. Jesus said, "Father, forgive them, for they do not know what they are doing" (Luke 23:34). It's true that some could argue from the context of this verse that the only people Jesus was referring to were the soldiers, since He made this statement immediately after they had driven the nails into His hands. But a closer look at the passage can also give credence to a broader application of His words to all the people surrounding Him. Regardless, Jesus gave grace to the vulnerable surrounding Him, even when He had bigger issues on His mind.

And what about the thieves who were crucified on either side of Him? You would think, what with the sins of the entire world on His shoulders, that He'd ignore these men. When you add to the equation that both men joined the crowd in hurling insults at Him,[1] you would think He would have been justified to view these two condemned men as mere footnotes of history—little more than simple props hanging on either side of Him to strike a greater contrast to the magnificence of His sacrifice. But that's not how Jesus' heart works.

Apparently, one of the thieves figured this out. His theology was crude, and his understanding was limited, but he figured out enough in his debilitated state. He figured out that Jesus was a King, just like the sign above His head read. He figured out that His kingdom wasn't of this world. And He believed that Jesus had the power to transport him to that kingdom after they both died. It was a primitive grasp of the salvation message. He called on Jesus by name, saying, "Jesus, remember me when you come into your kingdom" (Luke 23:42).

This thief couldn't have known that when they were being laid down side by side to be crucified Jesus already knew his name. Jesus could have told him how many hairs were on his head—not that he would have cared much at the moment. But Jesus already knew him that well. He could have told this thief things that no one else knew about him; things that would have demonstrated just how precious he already was to God. In the midst of His pain, His personal focus, His preoccupation with taking on the sins of the world, Jesus responded to this man's faith: "I tell you the truth, today you will be with me in paradise" (Luke 23:43).

Soldiers, leaders, followers, and criminals got Jesus' individual attention when He had bigger tasks on His "to do" list. That's because God's grace notices vulnerable people. It's in constant tune with their hearts.

This really hits close to home when you look at how Jesus dealt with His mother. Mary, this precious woman who had been singled out to provide a womb for the Redeemer, stood near the foot of the cross. She was flanked by Jesus' aunt and several faithful friends. Because she was in safe and good company, Jesus could have easily ignored her, focusing on His own grave situation instead. It would have been fair for Him to assume that because of who she was, and whom she was with, she would no doubt find adequate care after He died. But He was not just the only begotten Son of God, He was also the oldest son of Mary. His earthly guardian—Joseph, his mother's husband—was dead. He knew that His other brothers were going to have their hands full after His resurrection.[2] As the firstborn, it was Jesus' responsibility to leave instructions for her care since He had been condemned to die.

In the midst of His agony, Jesus noticed how vulnerable His mother would become as a result of His death. He might have had the world on His shoulders, but He focused enough to put His mother on His heart. His grace was specific, clear, and thorough. "When Jesus saw his mother there, and the disciple whom he loved [John] standing nearby, he said to his mother, 'Dear woman, here is your son,' and to the disciple, 'Here is your mother.' From that time on, this disciple took her into his home" (John 19:26–27).

None of these people could see what Jesus could see. None of them had any grasp of the bigger picture. Their needs were the result of their myopic condition, or their naiveté, or their lack of sophistication. Jesus could have dismissed their needs because of how small they appeared next to the bigger task before Him. But His grace kicked in, and it will kick in for us whenever we're feeling vulnerable. It also kicks in when we don't even realize just how vulnerable we actually are.

Our children need this kind of grace. Their confusing lives cry out for our sensitive touch. God gives us just enough of a head start to bring perspective and understanding to the fragile needs of our kids.

2. We need to give our children the freedom to be vulnerable because of the unique nature of childhood.

The position our children hold early in their lives makes them an automatic victim of two colliding forces inside them. On one side are the *facts* of any given situation. These are either the empirical particulars that can be quantified in an almost scientific way, or the abstracts that can be proved beyond a reasonable doubt. These are the things parents can see that our children can't always see.

On the other side of the equation are the *feelings* of any given situation. These often determine what our children perceive about the situation they're in. The key point is that the way our children feel about situations might not have any connection whatsoever to the facts. For instance, they may feel lonely, even though they have plenty of friends who dearly love them. They may feel unattractive, even though they're runway model material. They may feel fairly dim, even though their IQ tests say they're pretty smart. They may feel very inadequate with people and relationships, even though their teachers and youth group leaders have noticed their magnetic personalities and leadership skills that make others desirous to follow them. Because of this disconnect between the facts and the feelings, our children can feel extremely vulnerable as they move through their childhood.

It would be easy to dismiss their concerns with a simple recitation of the facts. But children's feelings have the power to cloud the facts. Regardless of what we point out, their hearts are often stuck in the "feelings" mode (just as we often are as adults). Their lack of maturity makes it hard for them to see beyond their emotions. The good news is that their problems dissipate as they grow older and have more experiences to help them filter their lives through, but not completely.

Healthy adults, unlike "Mr. Spock" (à la *Star Trek*), who has no capacity to emote, have the ability to *feel* with their emotions *as well as* make decisions based on truth and fact. One of the great factors that determine whether children grow up to be these kinds of healthy adults (i.e., adults who are not dominated and manipulated by their feelings) is how their vulnerabilities are handled when they are children. If children grow up in homes where their parents don't notice their vulnerabilities, don't acknowledge their vulnerabilities, or don't allow their vulnerabilities to come to the surface, these are the very children who could live out the rest of their lives as hostages to these areas of weakness.

> Regardless of what we point out, their hearts are often stuck in the "feelings" mode .

Grace-based homes are a vital link to children's wholeness and wellness as adults. That's because our vulnerabilities have the power to define us if we aren't careful. Legalism, strident or rigid parenting models, and preoccupied moms and dads can keep children from growing beyond their vulnerabilities. Grace is the key that unlocks the door to a balanced adult life.

Your willingness and ability to come alongside your children's vulnerabilities with grace helps them work through their difficulties. They might be afraid that you could be getting a divorce simply because many of their friends' parents have. You need to gracefully help them through this. They might be insecure because you or your spouse were married to someone else before. You need to acknowledge those fears and work overtime to help them process the effect your divorce had on them. They might feel stupid, foolish, gangly, out of place, or out of touch. They need a grace that offers love instead of lectures, understanding instead of ignorance, and a plan instead of a dismissal.

I DON'T WANT TO SOUND LIKE A SKIPPING CD, BUT . . .

When children feel the most vulnerable, it's almost always because one of their three driving inner needs is on trial. Sometimes it's all three at once. That's why it is critical for grace-based parents to make meeting these three inner needs their *daily* goal. These needs will always be in the present tense with your children. When they sense, for whatever reason, they aren't feeling secure, significant, or strong enough for the moment, a foreboding sense of vulnerability often overwhelms them. This can happen when they are infants in their cribs or high-school seniors ready for graduation. Whether your strapping son stands head and shoulders above his peers, or your gorgeous daughter sets the standard for elegance among her friends, all children find themselves looking down the barrel of insecurity, insignificance, or inadequacy.

This is exactly when the forces of darkness like to move in for the kill and explains why you cannot afford to trivialize these times when your children feel fragile. Satan doesn't. Actually, he loves it when they feel vulnerable. He traffics in counterfeit solutions to these needs. If you don't step forward with the love, purpose, and hope they need to compete with these challenges, Satan will. Actually, he will whether you offer these things or not. But Satan is no match for the grace of God. Children with parents who find their ultimate love, their profound purpose, and their supernatural hope in Jesus Christ have parents who can show them how to face their vulnerabilities with a love that is secure, a purpose that is significant, and a hope that is strong.

SPEAKING OF STRONG . . .

We've looked at part of this passage before. The apostle Paul knew what it was like to feel vulnerable. When you read his autobiography in 2 Corinthians 11, you realize that he had to process a lot of situations that caused him to question his sense of security, significance, and strength. In fact, the biggest tests to these inner needs happened *after* he gave his heart over to Christ for safekeeping.

Let me share a few of the high points (or low points) from his résumé:

> I have worked much harder, been in prison more frequently, been flogged more severely, and been exposed to death again and again. Five times I received from the Jews the forty lashes minus one. Three times I was beaten with rods, once I was stoned, three times I was shipwrecked, I spent a night and a day in the open sea, I have been constantly on the move. I have been in danger from rivers, in danger from bandits, in danger from my own countrymen, in danger from Gentiles; in danger in the city, in danger in the country, in danger at sea; and in danger from false brothers. I have labored and toiled and have often gone without sleep; I have known hunger and thirst and have often gone without food; I have been cold and naked. Besides everything else, I face daily the pressure of my concern for all the churches. Who is weak, and I do not feel weak? Who is led into sin, and I do not inwardly burn? (2 Corinthians 11:23c–29)

Anytime I find myself feeling sorry for myself, I turn to 2 Corinthians 11 to put my life back into perspective. I don't know of any other adult who was trying to live his life for Jesus Christ who had to pay a higher price over a prolonged period of time than Paul. I'm sure there are a few out there, but I don't know of them. What stirs my spirit when I read this passage is Paul's enthusiasm for the life God had given him. There's no whining, no raging, and no quitting. In fact, what this led him to was a profound sense of joy. What's also interesting is that none of his willingness to endure released him from the ongoing battle that everyone has with their weaknesses and temptations.

But Paul prevailed, and grace was the reason.

Lest you think I'm drawing a general assumption about this so that it can support the theme of this book, look at what follows this passage. A few verses later, Paul takes us deeper into the recesses of his soul, a peek at the profound pain he lived with and how he ultimately learned to cope with it through the grace of God.

Apparently, there was some point in Paul's adult life where he died. At least there seems to be an event that caused the separation of his soul from his body. If you recall, in his résumé he said, "Once I was stoned." There's a good chance that this was when he actually died. You can read about it in Acts 14:19. In the city of Lystra, this Scripture says, "Then some Jews came from Antioch and Iconium and won the crowd over. They stoned Paul and dragged him outside the city, thinking he was dead."

One thing about a public stoning was how effective it was at ending your life. Paul may have actually died here. Even he is not sure (2 Corinthians 12:2–3). Regardless, at some point in his adult life, God brought him up to heaven and let him take a good look at what was there. He heard things and saw things that man is not allowed to tell people on earth (2 Corinthians 12:4). God wanted to encourage Paul to keep up the battle. He had more than his fair share of reasons to give up. So God showed him what was awaiting him when his time on earth was finally done. This was a tremendous act of grace. Any time we can help people gain perspective in the midst of confusion, worry, doubt, or pain, we're giving them a gift.

But having seen all this could have sent Paul back into the battle with some conceit in his heart. He might have wanted to brag about his special treatment and spout off about what he had seen. After all, you can't name any of his contemporaries who got a backdoor tour of heaven led by God Himself. That's why God gave him a *problem* to contend with that would be a regular reminder to keep quiet and stay humble. "There was given me a thorn in my flesh, a messenger of Satan, to torment me," he says (2 Corinthians 12:7).

There's great debate as to what this thorn or messenger was, but the imagery tells us all we need to know. Whatever it was, it stung, burned, and throbbed like a thorn stuck under the skin. Remember the last time a rosebush got you? A thorn causes so much discomfort that you can't concentrate on anything else. You just want to stop everything and yank it out. That is apparently how this form of torment affected Paul, who also called it a messenger from Satan. Assuming that Satan would never be a bearer of glad tidings, this "thing" that God allowed into Paul's life apparently was some annoyingly painful reminder that was capable of bringing out the worst in him.

> My grace is sufficient for you, for my power is made perfect in weakness.
> (2 Corinthians 12:9)

Paul did what any of us would do. He approached God and begged for relief. This thorn in his flesh weakened him and showed him how vulnerable he really was. He pleaded with God three times to take it away. That means, for those of you keeping score at home, that after hearing the word "No!" from God once, he decided he wouldn't take "No!" for an answer. But after the third time, God added a caveat that helped Paul get through his affliction. He said:

> My grace is sufficient for you, for my power is made perfect in weakness. (2 Corinthians 12:9)

It was in God's grace that Paul figured out how to feel secure, significant, and strong. His personal weaknesses and points of vulnerability weren't removed, but he had the necessary grace to face them and accept them.

Sometimes God deliberately puts things in our children's lives that make them feel extremely fragile—and He doesn't take them away.

Maybe it's a son who's physically short and will always be that way. Maybe it's a daughter who's fighting the battle of the bulge and can never lose the extra pounds. Maybe it's a child who has some physical handicap or intellectual blind spot. They may be children chosen last and who will *always* be chosen last. Often God puts these very things in their lives as touch points for His grace. The best delivery system for this is a grace-based parent. Your love and understanding can be the very things that help your children turn these setbacks into setups.

That's what happened to Paul. Look how he concluded this discussion about his vulnerabilities:

> Therefore I will *boast* all the more gladly about my weaknesses, so that Christ's power may rest on me. That is why, for Christ's sake, *I delight in weaknesses*, in insults, in hardships, in persecutions, in difficulties. *For when I am weak, then I am strong.* (2 Corinthians 12:9b–10, emphasis mine)

You'll probably never know the profound impact that the giving of grace will have on your children's vulnerabilities, but it's obvious how much devastation can be wrought if you don't. If God had not visited Paul with grace during his times of vulnerability, his letters and his history probably would have turned out quite differently. It's the same for your children. Those things within their lives that give them pause are the very things you are called to meet with grace. There's no telling just how profound an effect your gift of grace will have in their lives.

ONE DAY THAT CHANGED EVERYTHING

The summer between my eighth- and ninth-grade years was a threshold that led to the front door of adulthood. When I had walked out the front door of my junior high school that June, I was awash with the anticipation of attending one of the largest and most prestigious high schools in the state. That's what you think when you know nothing about any of the other high schools. All I knew was come fall, I would walk the halls of Annapolis High School. My plan was to go out for the football team—one of the best teams in the county. They had almost a decade of victories to show for it. At the big high school, the girls were prettier, the rock-'n'-roll was louder, and the action more nonstop.

When school started in September, though, they didn't have enough room for all the new freshman students. To alleviate this problem, the administration annexed an elementary school about a mile away from the high school and shipped a couple of hundred of us freshmen to this building, which sat just a block from the city docks in the heart of Annapolis. I was one of those lucky freshmen, which meant I got to share a pint-sized campus with hundreds of screaming little kids half our size.

What a drag! We lacked a sophisticated library, elaborate science facilities, and had only limited classes in music and the arts. In my mind, though, the greatest sacrifice we made was in sports. We couldn't "dress out" for PE classes, which meant we had to play sports in our school clothes. That fall, we played flag football on the edge of a children's playground, and when winter arrived, we played basketball in a small gymnasium on the second floor of a county building a block away. No showers before we went back to class, which meant we spent the rest of the school day in smelly clothes.

One winter morning, I and my classmates walked the block to the nearby gym and climbed the stairs to the second floor where we found a trampoline set up in the middle of the basketball court. I had never jumped on a trampoline before.

When the bell rang to mark the beginning of our class, our gym teacher came out of his office and onto the court. He was the youngest teacher I had, fresh from college in his first assignment as a physical education instructor. He walked up to the trampoline and blew his whistle. That was the signal for all of us to stop what we were doing, shut up, and gather around. We made a solid rectangle of freshman boys ready to jump.

The teacher's eyes made a slow pass around the trampoline, studying each one of us. After he had looked at the last student, he looked back over at me and said, "Kimmel, take off your shoes, leave on your socks, climb up on the trampoline, and follow my instructions." I untied my shoes and climbed up onto the trampoline, but as I did, I noticed that I had holes in both socks. Normally, I wouldn't have thought much of it, but then one of my friends noticed.

"Check out the holes in Kimmel's socks! Hey, Tim, you want to borrow a pair of mine? Stop by my house on the way home, and I'll give you a pair. I've got plenty. Or maybe you'd prefer that we take up a collection for you after class."

"Knock it off!" the coach said, but the damage had been done. The guys had a good laugh, and they continued to make wise remarks even after the coach told them to be quiet.

You need to know a few things that will put this scenario in context. First of all, if this happened to me *now*, I could care less. I have the seasoning of years and the maturity that enables me to ignore teasing statements that my friends make—even laugh at them. But when you are in that corridor of time called adolescence, it is not uncommon to be overly sensitive about these kinds of things. This is a time when kids suffer from what I call "center stage syndrome." They are certain that *everyone* is noticing things about them. They are self-conscious about their looks, their social abilities, their intellect, and their economic situation. Kids at this age are *positive* that someone's looking at their ears or their nose or some other body part.

In this particular scenario, the put-downs drew attention (at least in my fragile way of reasoning) to my family's economic status. We were a family on the lowest rung of the middle class. We weren't what people would consider poor, but we wouldn't have been considered a family who had anything extra. We never missed a meal, though, and Dad and Mom managed to pay their bills on time. When it came to clothing, our family's philosophy was, "Get as much mileage out of your clothing as you can." Up to that point, I had thought that was a fairly good plan, but during my time on the trampoline, all I could think about were my toes sticking out of my socks and my fellow classmates snickering at the sight.

When I was done, the other kids in my class took their turns jumping on the trampoline. I never saw them jump up and down. All I could think about were my socks. *I'm going to go home and darn every sock that I have,* I thought. *I'll never allow something like this to happen to me again, ever!*

When the class was finally over, our PE teacher dismissed us to walk back to school, and he headed back to his office. I put on my shoes, careful to pull the tips of my socks down over my toes, and laced them up. I gathered my books from the stage at the end of the gym and started to head down the stairs to my next class. "Kimmel, wait up!" It was my PE teacher. He came bounding down the stairs, pulled me over into a little alcove and stepped close enough to me so that no one would be able to overhear.

"Tim, I wanted to tell you why I called on you to do that demonstration today in class. It's because I think you're the most agile student in my class." Then he untied one of his tennis shoes and pulled it off. The tip of his sock had a pronounced hole in it, and two of his toes were sticking out. He held his foot about halfway up, wiggled his toes, and said, "Us agile guys are tough on socks!" Then he put down his foot, started to put his tennis shoe back on, and said, "Now, go to class."

As I walked away, one question kept tumbling over and over in my head. *What's agile?* I had never heard the word before (which gives you an idea of what a pathetic student I was). But my next class was English, and that day I opened the oversized dictionary that sat on its stand and looked up the word *agile*. Out of the corner of my eye, I could see my English teacher grinning. She *loved* students who looked up words without her prompting.

I eventually found *agile,* and I read for the first time that I could "move with speed, ease, elegance, and liveliness." I also read for the first time that I was "mentally alert and quick witted."

No one had ever told me anything like this before. I wrote down that definition and read and reread it until I had memorized it. This incident changed my life in two vital areas. One of those areas was athletics. Two weeks later, the gym teacher had a contest to see who could do the most sit-ups in the ninth grade. I set the record at 560 sit-ups. These were full-on sit-ups where someone holds down your feet, and your legs stay flat on the floor while you come up and touch your elbows on the opposite knees. They don't even allow kids to do these kinds of sit-ups anymore because of how hard they are

In fact, my stomach muscles hurt for a week. But I didn't care, because I was agile.

on your back. In fact, my stomach muscles hurt for a week. But I didn't care, because I was *agile*.

I also made a transformation in my attitude as a student. Up to that point, I had been told I was average, and I had been placed in classes with average kids. But I suddenly saw my mind as I saw my body—as something capable of far more than I had originally thought.

It took me a while to put all the pieces together. I remembered how quickly my PE teacher had left after he dismissed us. That's because he raced to his office, pulled off his shoe, got out his scissors, cut a hole in his sock, put his shoe back on, and then caught up with me. He didn't go around with holes in his socks; he was a physical education teacher, for crying out loud.

But one morning he saw a vulnerable student, badly needing grace, and he gave him a gift. This young coach, fresh out of college, was paying attention to an area that most would have ignored. He saw an awkward kid in an embarrassing situation and realized how much it hurt. He empathized long enough to put himself in my shoes—and socks. He took action.

In that action he met my need for security. He showed me how loved and cared for I was. My PE teacher had gone out of his way to single me out and honor me with help for my heart. He also met my need for significance. In telling me I was agile, he was telling me that I had a gift most of my fellow students didn't have. This gift gave me a purpose outside of being average. He was telling me that I had already developed it in such a way that it was enabling me to stand out from the rank and file. He also met my need for strength. That someone noticed my physical abilities and intellectual prowess gave me hope for a more successful future. He was not only telling me what I was, but he was giving me reason to believe that I could be much more.

And I'm the better one for it.

Sometimes it's an ongoing challenge that shows up as one of a child's vulnerabilities. Other times it's a momentary sense of being overexposed that does it. Whatever it is, and whenever it is, our children need to know that it won't cost them to be vulnerable around us. In their weakness they need to find the path to true strength. God has given us stewardship over these wonderful opportunities to make a difference in our children's lives.

It's called grace-based parenting.

CHAPTER 9

The Freedom to Be Candid

Candid Camera is a show almost as old as television. It's gone through several incarnations and new hosts over the years, but is still basically the same gimmick. Ever since Allen Funt caught his first victim off guard back in 1953, this show has been placing people in confusing, embarrassing, and often hilarious situations that frequently bring out the worst in them. That's why I've always felt that this show should have had a different title. It's not really a *candid* camera, but something more like an *ambush* camera. The viewing audiences were in on the joke, Allen Funt and his production staff who set up the situation obviously knew about it, but the poor sap they trapped on camera didn't see it coming.

Sometimes the contrived dilemma caused people who were normally careful about the words coming out of their mouths to swear like a longshoreman. Or maybe they caught grandma-types known for their peaceful and quiet demeanor who then flew off the handle and delivered finger-pointing lectures. Then there were the so-called "pillars of the community" caught with their hands in the cookie jar.

So America laughed, but we also breathed a sigh of relief, glad it was them caught on national TV and not us. We don't know what we would do if we suddenly found ourselves in these same situations, but we know one thing for certain: We wouldn't want twenty million households peeking in when we found out. It requires only a basic knowledge of our limitations to realize that when our guard is down, there is no way to predict what we'd say, feel, or do in an awkward situation. We'd like to go through life knowing that should a situation like that come along, there aren't any video cameras ready to let America see how weak we are under pressure.

THE PROBLEM WITH HOneSTY

Everyone would agree that it's a good idea to be honest. Truthfulness and forthrightness are anchor tenets of quality character. These qualities glisten when they are used to report on things that can be weighed or measured empirically. But when these qualities are processed through the filter of a person's subjective perceptions, truth and forthrightness can just about kill. The problem with honesty is how "honest" it can actually be. What was meant to be a gift to relationships can turn out to be its poison pill.

When honesty is placed at the mercy of one's feelings, grace is often forced out of the picture. That's because when people express their honest *feelings*, they are filtering them through their past scars, their current hurts, their limited knowledge of the facts, and their bent toward self-protection. That's what you see when you tune into one of those brawls so popular on the Jerry Springer–type shows in the late afternoon. On these shows, broken people live out their broken lives in front of a studio audience. Everybody participates in a no-holds-barred verbal (and sometimes physical) slugfest. It's an excellent example of toxic honesty—forthrightness out of control. Honesty about what one person thinks of another person's life choices, looks, weight, or intelligence becomes high entertainment for people who should know better. These voyeuristic looks into the inner lives of dysfunctional families make some people feel better simply by giving them an example of others who are worse off than they are. But for too many of the people watching, these are concentrated examples of the honesty they deal with day in and day out.

That's why we need candor and not just honesty when it comes to the family. Candor isn't about catching people off guard to make them look worse than they are. Candor is several steps above honesty and is a way of communicating freely without prejudice or malice. Candor takes the truth and frames it in a way that helps rather than harms. There's also a high degree of *fairness* brought to bear within the true definition of candor. The most important nuance of candor is that it is supposed to be free of deception.

GRACE-BASED HOMES AND CANDOR

The third characteristic of grace-based homes is this: They are homes that give children the freedom to be candid. These are homes where what is on a child's mind can end up as dinner dialogue without fear of payback. That's because homes with candor create give-and-take between parents and children that promotes honesty dipped in honor. This is the next logical step in the creation of a grace-based environment.

> The third characteristic of grace-based homes is this: They are homes that give children the freedom to be candid.

Homes that encourage children to be different and vulnerable are homes where children are free to speak openly without fear that they will have their heads handed back to them on a stick. Grace makes the difference because it keeps honesty from getting ugly. It ratchets up the free exchange of heartfelt things to a much higher level of forthrightness—a *careful* forthrightness that guards the other person's dignity.

185

Grace-based candor is a road trip through the truth that keeps you from destroying each other along the way.

We need to create homes where we talk about the deep and sometimes troubling issues concerning our children in a way that builds them up and makes them better people. We also need to create environments where our children have the freedom to do the same with us, and this applies to their disappointments *in* us as well. Kids have questions about their sexuality as they get older. They need to feel free to discuss *anything* with us that might be troubling without embarrassing them or sensing that it will cost them more than it's worth. In our weak moments, we might do something that angers them or humiliates them or crushes their spirit. Grace-based homes provide an outlet where the children can respectfully voice their disappointment without fear of reprisals.

Regardless of how carefully you've developed your child's spiritual lives, some children go through times where their faith implodes. This might be a time when they doubt some things about God. They may feel adrift or entertain frightening spiritual alternatives. These children are far safer working through these important issues where grace is in place—in your home. They need parents who remain calm, spend time on their knees, and maintain an open forum where their children can work through their faith out loud.

I can walk you up to a particular house in Oregon, rap on the front door, and introduce you to two people who had to do all these things I have listed, and many more. This father and mother could easily qualify as the poster parents for grace-based homes. All of their three daughters were standouts—smart, talented, pretty girls who were raised to care more about others than about themselves. An interesting situation occurred, however, when circumstances dictated that their family relocate from Texas to the Pacific Northwest. The problem was that their youngest daughter was heading into her senior year in high school. When children are in the upper years of high school, it's almost never a good time to relocate. Some people have the flexibility or alternatives that allow them to wait until the child graduates. These folks didn't.

The move put their youngest daughter into an emotional tailspin. She was bitter about the decision that had ripped her away from her lifelong friends. Her new high-school situation left her feeling aimless and isolated. Her anger became real, personal, and focused—and this was a girl who had modeled a spiritual passion for Christ since early childhood. She didn't scream and yell and slam doors or pout, however. She had been raised well, so she continued to show respect for her parents' authority. She maintained a reasonable level of civility, but at the same time, a distinct, morose spirit came over her. It was as though she was shriveling up and dying spiritually inside.

Apparently, the uprooting of her family had torn away some of the key roots of her faith. Doubts crept in. Pretty soon, they took over. Each day brought new tears and a new set of questions about spiritual issues that her parents thought she had always embraced. Her faith evaporated so much that she couldn't even pray. Her Bible went on her shelf and stayed there.

It would be easy to say that this was an attempt to get even with her folks. Her father was in a ministry position at a college. Having a daughter in spiritual rebellion couldn't have been easy on him. Her parents could have seen her behavior as a passive attempt to control them or as a melodramatic show designed to punish them for the move.

But it wasn't any of these things. She had really taken a spiritual nosedive. One of the leading proofs that this was more than her punishing her parents for moving her away from her friends was in how quickly she recovered from the relocation. Because she was so smart, social, and athletic, she found herself well connected to a new set of friends by Christmas. By graduation, it was as though she'd been going to school with these students all her life, but her spiritual doubts only got worse. Even after her adjustments to her new surroundings, she still hadn't invited Jesus to join her in her new life in the Pacific Northwest. Her faith seemed to be completely gone.

Two items in her mom and dad's parenting philosophy helped her process her spiritual free fall—grace and candor. Her mother and father had always maintained an atmosphere of grace in a home not measured by rules or ruled by fears. Darcy and I have known this family since before they gave birth to this daughter we're talking about. Their girls had been provided a gracious environment in which to establish their relationship with Christ. The dynamic that her parents created within their home enabled this daughter to grieve her spiritual losses in the open. Her parents made it as comfortable as possible for her to "continue to work out [her] salvation with fear and trembling" (Philippians 2:12). She spoke of her disappointment with God, with the church, with individual Christians she knew, with them, and with her sisters. She voiced her doubts about the deity of Jesus, the validity of the Scriptures, and the genuineness of God's love.

She talked. They listened. She questioned. They listened and prayed. She cried. They cried. And this went on for well over a year. Sometimes it takes much longer. They trusted God for a good outcome, but their fears almost got the best of them. They knew where some of her doubts could lead her—down paths that ended up in philosophical, relational, and even sexual quicksand. But her parents maintained a steady stream of love, patience, and understanding. And finally, she came to some conclusions that led to a far deeper and richer faith than she had ever experienced back in Texas. In fact, she came to the conclusion that the reason she was put through her painful displacement was so that God could show her how much her faith had been propped up by the setting she had enjoyed in Texas. He also wanted to show her His grace.

> Grace-based families make room for their kids' opinions.

Grace-based families make room for their kids' opinions. They provide a safe forum in which to air their doubts, disappointments, and even their misguided beliefs. They especially provide an outlet for candor when their children's faith is on trial.

Strident, unadaptable Christian homes have no clue what this looks like. They have rules that have to be kept and an image that has to be propped up. These are families that have distilled their faith down to a short stack of platitudes that stick like Post-it notes on the inner walls of their souls. These are not homes that encourage candor. They lead with critique and allow no rebuttal. Children in strident Christian homes have neither a voice nor a vote. For these parents, it's their way (but certainly not "God's Way") or the highway. If you ever want to know how to close down your children's hearts to the deeper issues of the Spirit, just trade authentic faith for the cheap imitation that strident, graceless parenting has to offer. My friend's daughter wouldn't have stood a chance trying to process her doubts had she lived in such a spiritually limited home. She would have paid a heavy price, and most likely would still be paying it.

Fear-based families can't offer much either. Because this style of parenting functions in a reactive mode to the culture, there is little room for dialogue on questionable issues and doubtful topics—at least not straight-from-the-heart, transparent dialogue. As children move up through the layers of childhood development, there is an uneasiness in their spirits with broaching subjects that may bring these intimidating issues too close to the inner sanctuary of their "safe-based" homes. They know that their homes are anything but safe places to voice concerns about overbearing religion, underperforming spirituality, or alternative views about how to deal with their culture. It's not that their parents don't care. Actually, these are some of the most well-intended parents one could find. It's just that fear-based homes operate as though to even *discuss* biblical alternatives to the parents' strict ways of dealing with the cultural challenges that bombard their children is on par with letting these cultural challenges define the family. When you understand the role of God's grace in tempering a family, then you realize that this fear-based assumption could not get much farther from the truth.

TOXIC BLUNTNESS

Then there are what I call lawless homes. Kids trying to work through the more touchy issues of the heart have absolutely no chance of getting any help from these homes. Because these families often lack an uncompromising commitment to clear moral convictions, candor seldom gets a chance to operate within their walls. You just get a blunt and ruthless honesty based on how an individual *feels*, and the inaccurate readings that come from having a moral compass that must subordinate to these feelings.

Let me give you an example of a family that was seriously scarred by this kind of toxic bluntness. But first, let me introduce the one who will tell you her story. Jamie is a sweet, decent lady who married an irresponsible, selfish man. I realize that most women figure that's what they've married after a few days into their honeymoon. But a lot of husbands grow into good men. Jamie's didn't. He was a man with layers of problems. One of them was the way he spoke exactly what was on his mind, but with no regard for how it affected the person on the receiving end of his "honesty." Before he was through, he'd imprinted his toxic ways onto his children. I want you to also notice how his heartless rebuff of his ten-year-old son played a huge role in sending this boy into a moral free fall. At a time when his boy was lovingly trying to talk to his dad about a huge concern he had regarding him, his father fired back with exactly what was on his mind. In many ways this is a forthright father—but lacking any commitment to temper his honesty with anything remotely resembling grace.

And caught in the middle of this ongoing nightmare was a wife and mother who felt helpless. She's a good example of how injured feelings and huge disappointments can cause a person to ignore their internal moral compass when under stress. She is, no doubt, also a woman who had no help from her parents in establishing a clear sense of security, significance, and strength in the core of her heart. Before it was over, one man's unbridled bluntness cost an entire generation of his offspring their self-respect. What follows are Jamie's actual words:

My son, Martin, does not have a relationship with his dad at all. His dad is very critical and condescending. He tells him that he will never be anything and that he will end up in the grave or in prison. He's heard these kinds of blunt appraisals from his father ever since he was a little boy. It's strange how when Martin was ten years old, he found marijuana in his dad's toolbox, and he confronted him about it. His dad literally spit in his face. I think that was a pivotal moment in Martin's life. A year later, I divorced his father after fifteen years of marriage. My kids were eleven and twelve years old.

At the time of this confrontation over the marijuana, I had actually thought things were looking up. I had found Christ several years earlier. I started praying that my husband, Chad, would find Jesus, too. I prayed that he would find a job with a Christian company, and he did. He didn't know it at the time, but he was working with men who had formerly spent years on the foreign mission field. The owner of the company even gave his testimony at a get-together one Christmas. I just believed that our little family would make it. I kept on believing that until Chad got to know the twenty-three-year-old assistant filling in for the main secretary at the company who was on extended sick leave. She filled in long enough to finish off what was left of our marriage.

I knew Chad was acting strangely, but it never dawned on me that he was having an affair. He asked me to come home from work one day and told me that he loved me like a sister. He denied that he was seeing someone. I found out the truth later. My son, Martin, witnessed this kind of flawed modeling of his father. I felt so bad for Martin. I filed for divorce. We moved out. I continued going to church. I cried a lot.

Martin morphed into a very angry boy. After his father and I divorced, he started getting into trouble at school almost every day. I was at my wit's end. Everything I tried fell short. I realize that out of guilt and shame, I felt I needed to cover for him. I know I made his life worse by getting him out of a lot of the consequences his actions deserved.

I met a guy in the "singles" department at my church. He had four sons. He seemed like a great guy . . . at the time. In my desperate state, I figured he would be good for Martin. We married. As it turned out, we all brought a lot of baggage to our new marriage. About all the blending our families have done was to make it easier for his kids and my kids to mutually corrupt each other. All of our children have been damaged by divorce.

One of his kids is in prison, and Martin should probably be there with him. Martin lives with his father, Chad. Martin has had problems with drugs. He has been in treatment. The good news is that he will be going into the Marine Corps this coming Tuesday. I love my son. I want the best for him. I'm sure I've enabled a lot of his behavior. I am in the process of letting go. I realize that Martin has to fall on his face and learn. I think the Marine Corps will be good for him. There are a lot of healthy grown men that can mentor him if he will just let them. I feel so guilty for getting married and further messing up Martin's life. Martin is leaving early Tuesday morning for boot camp at Parris Island, South Carolina. I'm hoping for the best.

For the record, the good sergeant down at the induction depot at Parris Island figured Martin out in about ten minutes. That marked the beginning and the end of Martin's career as a marine. Here was a boy who grew up on the receiving end of the graceless bluntness of his father. God didn't design the human heart to thrive in this kind of environment—especially not one that is so young and tender. Martin's sure hasn't.

Reading Jamie's story is like peeking at the *Jerry Springer Show*. You might think, *I guess we're not doing so badly after all. At least we're not that messed up.* But to think that is to diminish the humanity of Jamie, Martin, Chad, and the rest of the players in this extremely sad family. These are real people with real broken lives. They'd like to get their little bite of the "happy pie" just like everyone else. They just can't seem to figure out how.

These are not people to be looked down on but people to be pitied. They have no clue what grace looks like because it has never been part of the fabric of their key relationships. It wouldn't surprise me if the adults in this picture were dishonored by their own parents when they were growing up. Dishonor begets dishonor. Regardless, they are now living with the blinding effect of toxic honesty. All they seem to understand is an unbridled and unfiltered frankness. It's a skewed honesty that must slip through layers and layers of disappointments before it's turned into actual words. It makes it real hard to think straight.

> Dishonor begets dishonor. Regardless, they are now living with the blinding effect of toxic honesty.

In saying this, however, I am not absolving any of the people in this unfortunate discourse from responsibility for their actions. Not only are they fully responsible for what they've done and what they are doing, but when it's all said and done, they will have no one to blame but themselves.

DEGREES OF DIFFERENCE

One of the main reasons I think it's hard to look down on Jamie's family with an air of superiority is because in most cases Jamie's family is separated from your family and mine by only a few degrees. We might speak more kindly and dishonor less. We might lead more wisely and deceive less. But even the best families close children's spirits either by not encouraging the truth or by abusing it.

God knew that we are all capable of turning truth into a weapon of mass destruction. He gave us a contrast and a qualifier to keep the truth tempered in Ephesians 4:14–15:

> Then we will no longer be infants, tossed back and forth by the waves, and blown here and there by every wind of teaching and by the cunning and craftiness of men in their deceitful scheming. Instead, speaking the truth in love, we will in all things grow up into him who is the Head, that is, Christ.

God knew that when truth is unsheathed, it often has a razor's keen edge. Lives can be sliced to shreds with the simple dissemination of truth, the whole truth, and nothing but the truth. This kind of truth works well in courtrooms, but it can destroy relationships. The God of all truth and all love knew that we needed both these attributes of His divine character to keep us from filleting each other. Running truth through a filter of love moves honesty to the more others-oriented level of candor.

Earlier in this book, we defined *love* as "the commitment of my will to your needs and best interests, regardless of the cost." That means our honesty must be delivered with its effect on the other person in mind. We can't just spew out opinions and remarks. Grace requires that we deliver words about touchy subjects with a commitment to help—even heal—the other person. Grace requires that this commitment to speak the truth in a spirit of love works both ways—that we speak this way to our children and that we let them speak this way to us.

CHANGING LANES

I remember listening to a country song a long time ago with words that went something like this: "Love is a two-way street, but my baby's changing lanes." This happens, you know. Life throws us a slider, or we do something that puts the people we love at odds with us. It could be our four-year-old, our teenager, or our grown children. Kids have minds of their own, dreams of their own, fears of their own, and convictions of their own. From the day they are born, they begin the process of growing independent of us. As Christian parents, there are some issues—almost life-and-death issues—that we want to make sure they've decided on before they leave our sphere of influence. But we're not their only influence—just their biggest one. Since there are contrary forces also whittling away at their insides, we need to create an easy way for them to voice the cries of their hearts so we can help them process issues adequately.

Sometimes our children evaluate what they are learning from us by approaching our core convictions with an air of skepticism—especially when they are teenagers. Grace-based homes that allow a free exchange of candor-level honesty enable these kids to work through these convictions while feeling highly valued by us—even though we may disagree on several matters. When we don't provide this outlet, the most prominent alternative to their skepticism is full-scale rebellion. Many Christian families could have saved themselves the "prodigal years" if they had simply provided their children with a way to respectfully discuss their concerns and their confusions.

echoes WITHOUT MeRCY

Let's say that a kid in a Christian home wants to voice a contrary opinion about something he's trying to sort through. Or perhaps he needs to explain how his insides are responding to his parents' words or actions. Millions of these kids of churchgoing parents hear something like this in response:

- ➜ "I am the parent, you are the child. I outrank you. Therefore, be quiet."
- ➜ "If you don't like it, you can lump it."
- ➜ "Your feelings and concerns are not up for discussion."
- ➜ "I personally don't care what you think."
- ➜ "In fact, what you think is irrelevant."
- ➜ "You don't have a vote."
- ➜ "It doesn't matter how you see this."
- ➜ "Your opinion doesn't count."
- ➜ "We don't talk about those kinds of topics in this house."

Of course, you are the parent. You are in charge. You do have the final say and the ultimate authority. There are many times within the day-to-day workings of a family in which the children do not have a say or a vote. We're not addressing *those* kinds of issues here. For instance, bedtime is bedtime; it's not open for debate. What Mom cooks for the family is what you eat. A committee of children does not decide the daily agenda of a family—the parents do. We're not talking about *these* kinds of issues at this point.

Where children should feel free to speak up would be in those areas of their lives where they are wrestling with major moral issues, major relational issues, major spiritual issues, and major frustrations with us. Grace makes room for those areas.

> Grace makes room for them to tell us things about ourselves that we might not be excited to hear.

Grace makes room for them to tell us things about themselves that we might not be excited to hear. Grace makes room for them to voice their doubts and fears. Grace makes room for them to walk with us through adult issues they are struggling with. Grace makes room for them to tell us things about ourselves that we might not be excited to hear.

Let's say that a teenage son brings up the fact that he doesn't seem to have any success with girls. He's asked out a couple of girls over the past few months, and they've all rejected him. The girls don't seem to notice who he is. They seem more interested in his popular friends or the upper-classmen, but never him. He's wondering what all this means.

He may be wondering if he is gay. That's the thought the world would want him to entertain. He may even think it's a possibility. Let's say that he voices these thoughts about his sexuality to his father. If his father dismisses him with a terse, "Don't talk like an idiot," or something like, "You're imagining things. You're just thinking irrationally," and then makes that the end of the conversation, the boy could walk away from the best—and perhaps only—person in a position to give him wise and loving counsel. A curt or churlish response from his father could leave him feeling that it wasn't worth it to make himself that transparent to his dad. He's embarrassed *enough* about this, and he would rather not suffer any more humiliation at the hands of his father.

If this home were filled with grace, a son struggling with these kinds of worries would not only be welcomed to voice them but also applauded for doing it. His parents are in the best position to help him through these uncomfortable thoughts, and they should be grateful that he chose to share his heart with them rather than with someone who could steer him in the wrong direction.

This would be a great opportunity for his father to listen closely and ask questions. This would be a great time for his dad to tell of his own struggles with girls (assuming he had them). This is a time for a father to remind his son of some basic things about boy-girl relationships. He could remind his son that most girls tend to be ahead of boys in this department and that girls seem to go after the older guys during high school. This is a good time to encourage him in his masculinity and to affirm him about his future as a married man and a father. Kindness, understanding, and tender advice give a boy an overwhelming sense that he is not walking through these difficult times alone.

It's great when teenagers can discuss with us the frustrations they are having with their boyfriends or girlfriends, the disturbing conversations they have with friends, the things they are troubled about at school, and the spiritual battles they are fighting. But in listing these things, it would be easy to think that we're referring primarily to older children. Not so. Little kids need the freedom to be candid as well. When the smallest child in the house knows that she has a safe set of ears to tell her deepest concerns to, that child rests in the knowledge that she has parents who are committed to her success.

CAUGHT IN THE CROSS HAIRS

The most significant benefit of candor for our children can be the most painful to us. This happens when we allow our children to be forthright regarding how they feel about us. Most parents don't even give their children this option. Children in these types of homes are quick to figure out that their mother and father aren't interested in hearing their feelings about them. They aren't looking for an authentic relationship at the heart level with their children. It's common for these children to tell their parents what they want to hear rather than what is on their minds. This isn't the pursuit of truth but rather the careful airbrushing of an illusion.

Author Dr. Dan Allender speaks boldly about the value of honesty and the damage that is done when we don't encourage it:

> Honesty is the commitment to see reality as it is, without conscious distortions, minimization, or spiritualization. Honesty begins by admitting we are deceived, and that we would rather construct a false world than face the bright, searing light of truth. An honest person acknowledges his fondness for vague, half-truths that neither require change nor rip away the presumption of self-sufficiency.
>
> Why must we admit what is true? Because dishonesty, or living in denial, is actually an attempt to dethrone God. It is an attempt to become as God with the power to construct the world and reality according to our desire. A person committed to denying hard truths must construct an alternate world and, then, like Atlas, keep it spinning on [his or] her own power. The creation of a false world is really an attempt to shut God out of our world. It's much like the child who says, "Unless you play by my rules, I'll take my ball and bat and go home." God does not play by our rules nor resolve our wound and ache as we desire; therefore, we leave God's world and create one that is more palatable to our taste, even if it robs us of life and love.[1]

The unwillingness to give a voice to the hurts we have placed in our children's hearts is the epitome of high control. High-controllers are not strong people but rather weak, small, and selfish. In contrast, it is our openness to "openness" that draws us closer to our children's hearts and to God.

The relationship between God the Father and Jesus the Son is just one of the examples in the Bible that demonstrate this. Jesus came to do His Father's will. That meant *everything* His Father had sent Him to do. But when the moment came for the Savior of the world to complete His job, reality washed over Him. As Jesus stood on the threshold of the Crucifixion and knew that His time had finally come, He was overrun and overwrought by the price of it all. The scourging, the thorns, the nails, were just hours away. In that moment of humanness, the Son did what He knew He had the freedom to do any time with His Father. He slipped to the back corner of Gethsemane, fell to His knees, and had a candid heart-to-heart talk with His Dad.

We get to listen in on only half the conversation in the Gospels. We can tell the kind of reception He received from His Father by what Jesus said: "My Father, if it is possible, may this cup be taken from me" (Matthew 26:39).

I just can't hear the Father saying anything like, "A deal's a deal; stop Your whining!" In fact, just writing that made my heart hurt because there's nothing in God the Father's nature that would even hint He'd say such a thing—especially to His precious Son, who was willing to demonstrate so much love for others. But there are human fathers who dismiss their children's questions and doubts with statements far terser. They don't enjoy what was basic between Jesus and His Father.

Jesus came to do His Father's will and was committed to seeing it through. Ultimately, He said, "Yet not as I will, but as You will." He arrived at this place after His Father had listened to His pleadings and identified with His human reservations about what was about to happen. The Father didn't rebuke His Son for asking or begrudge Him for hoping for some way out. He just listened to His painful plea and came alongside Him with help for His resolve. They both knew there was no other way to redeem mankind.

Jesus came back to His Father a second time and a third time. The Father's love allowed His Son to wrestle with the same issue even though the facts were not going to change. That's because in the grace of the moment, the Father wanted to be available to His Son to listen as long as it took for Him to work through His anxiety.

THE EVIDENCE OF PRAYER

The relationship between Jesus and His Father demonstrates the wisdom of allowing candor in parent-child relationships. The fact that we are offered the option to *pray* also illustrates the high value God places on the priority of candor in His relationship with us. The writer of the book of Hebrews captured the beauty of our candid relationship with God almost too well. I say that because once you read what he wrote, there is no excuse for families to think they can operate any differently:

> Therefore, since we have a great high priest who has gone through the heavens, Jesus the Son of God, let us hold firmly to the faith we profess. For we do not have a high priest who is unable to sympathize with our weaknesses, but we have one who has been tempted in every way, just as we are—yet was without sin. Let us then approach the throne of grace with confidence, so that we may receive mercy and find grace to help us in our time of need. (Hebrews 4:14–16)

A person might say, "Yeah, these are great biblical points about letting people vent regarding the anxiety they are going through, but this doesn't say anything that justifies kids' voicing their disagreements with us as parents. God wouldn't allow that, would He? Jesus didn't do that to His Father. He brought His concerns and hurts to Him, but He did not try to tell His Father how to run His kingdom. What you're suggesting is that we give our children the freedom to voice even their disagreements with and disapproval in us. I don't think God would tolerate that."

Actually, you might be surprised what God would tolerate, even encourage.

The Place

Somewhere near the top of Mount Sinai.

The Scenario

God has been delivering His moral, civil, and ceremonial law to His servant Moses. The process has taken more time than the folks back at the base camp figured it would—or should. Because of his absence from the million-plus members of the children of Israel's camp, the people have started to second-guess why it is taking Moses so long to return. For all they know, he might not be coming back.

In a desire to take matters into their own hands, they ask Moses' brother, Aaron, to make them an idol who might have more going for it than this Almighty God that Moses is dealing with. Aaron has them cough up all their gold earrings from their wives, their sons, and their daughters (idolatry has an uncanny way of separating a family from their assets). Aaron melts the earrings down and shapes them into a golden calf. The result is that the people go nuts. They proceed to offer burnt offerings and sacrifices to the calf as well as savor the moment by turning the scene into a drunken orgy.

The Conflict

God interrupts His time with Moses to inform him that the people he left down at the bottom of the mountain have just popped a moral gasket. He tells Moses about the golden calf and the hedonistic worship service they are having. God is angry because these people have such short memories and such little devotion. They've quickly forgotten about the ten plagues, the Passover, the escape through the middle of the Red Sea, the drowning of Pharaoh's army, and the water from the rock. Listen to how God wants to solve the problem:

"I have seen these people," the LORD said to Moses, "and they are a stiff-necked people. Now leave me alone so that my anger may burn

201

against them and that I may destroy them. Then I will make you into a great nation. (Exodus 32:9-10)

I don't know about you, but if I were Moses, I would have felt that this was one of the best ideas God had come up with yet. *Nuke these spoiled, wicked brats, and start all over with me*, he could have thought. It would have been a simple way for God to deal with a huge problem. It would have saved Moses a lot of hassle, too.

But Moses loved those wicked, spoiled brats, and he knew that God loved them more than he did. Moses also loved God and didn't want God's reputation to suffer when He exploded in righteous anger toward these "stiff-necked" people. Here's how Moses responded to God's desire to destroy His chosen people:

"O LORD," he said, "why should your anger burn against your people, whom you brought out of Egypt with great power and a mighty hand? Why should the Egyptians say, 'It was with evil intent that he brought them out, to kill them in the mountains and to wipe them off the face of the earth'? Turn from your fierce anger; relent and do not bring disaster on your people. Remember your servants Abraham, Isaac and Israel, to whom you swore by your own self: 'I will make your descendants as numerous as the stars in the sky and I will give your descendants all this land I promised them, and it will be their inheritance forever.'" (Exodus 32:11b–13)

We need to understand the bigger picture of what was happening here. Moses had already seen God's mighty power. He had witnessed how much damage His death angel did to the firstborn sons of Egypt. He had watched the waters that God had separated come back together and drown Pharaoh's army. He'd seen the fierce thunder, felt the earthquake, and braced himself against the violent winds that encompassed Sinai. And yet he didn't hesitate to disagree with God and remind Him of the promise He had made to the Patriarchs. The reason he didn't hesitate to do this was because he knew he had the freedom to do it. He knew that in spite of all the other frightening features of Jehovah, He was still a God of grace.

The Outcome

Then the LORD relented and did not bring on his people the disaster he had threatened. (Exodus 32:14)

IT'S NOT JUST WHAT YOU SAY, BUT . . .

Even in the highest ranks of the military, there is an encouragement of those of lower rank to be candid with their superior officers. Soldiers do the most dangerous work on the globe. They kill the enemy while trying to keep themselves from getting killed. Because so much is at stake, everyone—down to the lowest ground-pounding grunt—has an outlet to respectfully voice concerns and point out vital information that might have been overlooked. The reason the military encourages this is because people in the lower ranks have so much to lose—like their lives. They also encourage new information because it could mean the difference between victory and defeat.

Our children's lives, their goals, and their dreams are also in our hands. So much is at stake for them. They have much to lose if we are moving ahead with bad plans. The difference between success and failure for us as parents could rest with the painful truth that we could hear from our children.

Grace-based families create respectful ways for children to voice these frustrations with their parents. Paul tells us what this looks like when it is done properly:

Let your conversation be always full of *grace*, seasoned with salt, so that you may know how to answer everyone. (Colossians 4:6, emphasis mine)

> Grace-based families create respectful ways for children to voice these frustrations with their parents.

Paul is encouraging us to not only saturate our words with grace, but to carefully weigh how they will affect the person on the receiving end. If you slide over in the Bible to the second half of Ephesians chapter 4, you'll find Paul giving specific instructions on how to handle conflict. This section of Scripture could easily be subtitled: "How to Fight Fairly." A couple of verses give us ample instruction on what the back-and-forth should look like between parents and children who have difficult things to say to each other:

> Therefore each of you must put off falsehood and speak truthfully to his neighbor, for we are all members of one body. "In your anger do not sin": Do not let the sun go down while you are still angry, and do not give the devil a foothold . . . Do not let any unwholesome talk come out of your mouths, but only what is helpful for building others up according to their needs, that it may benefit those who listen. And do not grieve the Holy Spirit of God, with whom you were sealed for the day of redemption. Get rid of all bitterness, rage and anger, brawling and slander, along with every form of malice. Be kind and compassionate to one another, forgiving each other, just as in Christ God forgave you. (Ephesians 4:25–27, 29–32)

The best way to ensure that our children will speak respectfully when they are voicing their disappointment or disapproval over something is to make sure that is exactly how we speak to them when it's the other way around. Parents are dreaming if they think they can dishonor their children, bark and bite when they are addressing them, and then get anything less in return. I've been on the inside of Christian families where I've heard parents speak more harshly to children who have committed minor infractions than judges speak to serial killers when they are reading them their verdicts and telling them why they are sentencing them to death. We need grace.

EATING CROW

Darcy and I figured out early that we were doing things that irritated our children. Even though we weren't always sure what they were, we figured we were doing things that ticked them off because Darcy and I did things that ticked *us* off. At the outset of our marriage, she and I established a practice of candor that could keep negative things from building up between us. We figured that method of communication worked so effectively for us, we could do the same with our kids.

We had a clear mandate from Scripture to spur us on—Hebrews chapter 12. The text refers to an incident in the Old Testament where Esau, Isaac's eldest son and Abraham's grandson, missed the blessing of the firstborn from his father. His younger brother Jacob had ripped him off through a ruse that he carried out with the help of his mother. Keep in mind that Esau was a piece of work even without the excuse of his deceiving younger brother. He had earlier scorned his birthright. He had let his sexual appetite, his penchant for pagan women, and his indifference to God dominate his life. Even so, when he realized that the words of favor and hope from his father were lost, he melted. The passage suggests that Esau *regretted* what he had done.

It says in verse 17: "Afterward, as you know, when he wanted to inherit this blessing, he was rejected. He could bring about no change of mind, though he sought the blessing with tears."

He could bring about no change of mind. The *New American Standard Bible* translates this "for he found no place for repentance." You can read the original story for yourself in Genesis 27. When you do, you'll notice there is no indication that Esau repented of anything. So how can the writer of Hebrews suggest that he did? The answer is a theological concept called "progressive revelation." It's an expression used to reconcile some of the insights that New Testament writers had when they commented on Old Testament events. They sometimes suggest things that don't appear in the original story because God gave them insider knowledge through the inspiration of the Holy Spirit. Apparently Esau tried to repent after the episode, but his parents did not provide an outlet for him to do that. It had to be a tragic and hopeless scenario for Esau. If this was indeed the case—that Isaac and Rebekah (Esau's parents) would not provide an outlet for the processing of his regret—then it is also a powerful reminder of the long-term, devastating effects that result when families don't provide a grace-based outlet for candor that leads to reconciliation. The offspring of Esau and Jacob continue to war today—thousands of years later. Terror and death have become the legacy of this family that refused to provide for graceful candor.

Just before this passage, in Hebrews 12:15 the writer says, "See to it that no one misses the grace of God and that no bitter root grows up to cause trouble and defile many."

My wife and I have met many people in our work who say something like, "My parents never once admitted that they did anything wrong." Often these have been people who grew up in patently Christian families. Darcy and I made it a commitment to make sure that years from now, should anyone inquire of our children as to whether we ever admitted our mistakes to them, they'd say, "Sure. Lots of times. In fact, all the time."

We wanted to not only make sure that we took responsibility for what we did wrong, but we wanted to also give them an outlet to bring to our attention things we might have missed. We didn't want the root of bitterness to find its way into the soil of our children's souls. We had already seen enough of that in our extended families. Please note that we did not do this because we were such wise and clever parents. Hardly. We did this because we were desperate. We had seen how much damage bitterness could do by working with so many angry families over the years. That's why we instituted "What's Your Beef?" nights.

While our children were still quite young, we came up with this vehicle to give them a safe way to air their disappointments. It was actually fairly simple. Periodically, we'd declare that tomorrow night would be a "What's Your Beef?" occasion. That meant, first of all, that each child could order whatever he or she wanted off the Kimmel menu. If one wanted Chinese, another Mexican, another Italian, and the other ribs, it was no problem. I just made the rounds of the nearby fast-food joints. The second part of the event provided them an opportunity to tell us anything that either Darcy or I had said or done that had hurt them. The qualification was that they couldn't bring up positions we had to take because of our moral standards (which they might have disagreed with) or consequences that we might have had to bring their way because of things they had done wrong. But they could address the way we handled taking our stand or bringing consequences down on them. It might have been harsh words or something we said that embarrassed them in front of their friends, or it could have been something we didn't do that they felt we should have done.

They would take turns to speak their minds. The key rule for Darcy and me when they shared these things from their hearts was that *we were not permitted to defend ourselves*. No matter what the issue, no matter how much insight we could employ to defend our position or our actions, we were not permitted to say a word in our defense. That was the promise we made, and the promise we kept.

Why did we choose not to defend ourselves? In any given crisis, there are the *facts* of the conflict and the *feelings* of the conflict. Depending on which way the parties look at the conflict, both are convinced that they are right and both are convinced that the other person is wrong. If my daughter or son was looking at a particular situation from the perspective of his or her feelings, I might have been able to justify my words or actions from my perspective of the facts, but it would have only done harm. The point was, we had hurt them somehow, regardless of the facts. This is how we handled the final part of the process. No matter what they said, and regardless of what we felt about the way they were viewing our actions, we asked for forgiveness. It was that simple. On occasion, we begged their pardon and forgiveness. It was often painful to hear how we had hurt them, and sometimes we had to fight the urge to clarify things. But we weren't doing it for our benefit; we were doing it for theirs.

An interesting phenomenon evolved from this group event, which started when our four children were young and small. Growing up, they assumed that they had the freedom to take advantage of this same opportunity any time they wanted. That was fine with Darcy and me. Several times I had one of my children pull me aside and say something like, "Dad, can I have a private 'What's Your Beef?' discussion with you?" I've treasured these as some of the most powerful opportunities to practice the grace of God.

SOMETIMES I'M REALLY DIM

My son Cody approached me on a Tuesday evening during the spring semester of his junior year of high school. The conversation (with commentary) went something like this:

Cody: Dad, I need you to call me out of school tomorrow at noon.
Me: And why would I do that?
Cody: My friend Steve has tickets to the opening game of the Diamondbacks.
(Commentary: We live in Scottsdale, Arizona, close to Phoenix. The year before, the Arizona Diamondbacks had won the World Series.)
Me: Son, listen. You're a student. You've got to go to school. You don't get to take off just because you want to go to a baseball game.
Cody: But Dad, Randy Johnson's going to be pitching.
Me: I don't care if Warren Spahn rises from the dead to pitch. You're a high-school student, and you're supposed to be in school.
Cody: Dad, Steve's got box seats right behind the Diamondbacks' dugout. There's going to be a flyover by F-18's. There are going to be a lot of festivities because they won the World Series last year, and there are going to be a lot of celebrities there.
Me: (This is when I decided to give him a little lesson in adult responsibility.) Listen, Cody, we all have jobs to do. You have a job. I have a job. My job is to get up and go to my office. I do my work.

I earn money to provide for the family. I don't get to skip work just because something fun comes along that I'd like to do. You are a student. You actually are getting paid to go to school. Your pay is the home and amenities you are provided that free you up to concentrate unencumbered on your education. Your job is to get up and go to school with a good attitude. You are to go there prepared for your day. You are supposed to pay attention, take good notes, show respect to your teachers, and work hard. When you come home at night, the continuation of your job is to do any homework you have been assigned. That's what you are supposed to do. That is what you are being paid to do. In real life, Cody, you don't get to take off whenever you feel like it just to go to a baseball game—regardless of the kind of seats you have.

Cody: (After a long pause and with an obvious feeling of frustration in his voice.) Dad, I bring home straight A's. I've brought home straight A's since kindergarten. I can't bring home any better grades than I'm bringing you. (Pause) You decide.

My little lecture about work and responsibility was exposed for what it was—just a bunch of hot air. Here was a boy who knew all about personal responsibility, doing his best, and working hard. He was an excellent student and a fine son. If anyone was setting a good pace and showing people around the house how to put forth a good effort, it was Cody. He was a good kid who simply wanted to go to an opening-day ball game. And he was leaving it up to his dimwitted, boneheaded father to have the last word and make the final call.

Me: (After first reaching into my pocket, pulling out a fold of money, and peeling off two $20 bills.) Make sure you buy yourself and Steve the big hot dogs and huge Cokes. Forgive me, son, for not seeing the obvious. Go have a great time. I'll be glad to get you excused.

Play ball!

CHAPTER 10

The Freedom to Make Mistakes

I don't know who originally said it, but someone decided a long time ago that home is where life makes up its mind. I think they were right—probably too right.

What happens inside the four walls of a family home does more to affect the outcome of children's lives than any other single factor. That's because of the nature of a family. It's the womb, the early nest, the home address, and the last name. Families create a group identity that defines everyone in that home individually. We may be one of a kind, but we're still a chip off the old block.

Because this is true, the people in charge of their children have a huge responsibility to pay attention to what they're doing. If you're sleepwalking through the defining factors of your children's lives, you can handicap their ability to be all that God meant them to be when they become adults.

Grace keeps you from tilting too far to one side or too far to the other. It works just like a carpenter's level. Grace helps you find the balance point in a world of extremes and keeps you from investing your energies in a long list of things that don't matter.

KEEPING THE BUBBLE IN THE MIDDLE

Grace provides equilibrium for a family. Where too many parents are concerned with how others view their children, grace-based parents are more excited with how God views their children. Grace-based parents avoid the silly preoccupations with arbitrary standards devised by evangelical busybodies. They keep their eye on the bubble in the level, which is their children's character. To them, keeping their children balanced when it comes to their faith, integrity, poise, discipline, endurance, and courage makes more sense than worrying about whether others think their children *look* spiritual enough (whatever that means). They don't make it a crime for their children to be different, to be oddballs, or to boogie to a different drumbeat. In the process, they encourage their children to find the unique individual that God designed them to be through an intimate and authentic relationship with Christ.

Grace doesn't make it uncomfortable for children to discover that they might not be that smart, talented, or clever. Parents who embrace grace make their homes a safe place for average kids to develop into extraordinary people. In these types of homes, weaknesses and inadequacies aren't a big deal. These families are overseen by shrewd mothers and fathers who see their children's fragile features as opportunities for God's power to shine through them. They also know that giving their children a safe place to work through their vulnerabilities keeps these shortcomings from getting in the way of their true greatness.

Homes configured by grace are not secret societies. Instead they are places where the parents aren't afraid to let their children voice what lies in the back rooms of their hearts. They even encourage them to cry out loud—even if it is about their disappointment with these same parents.

That's because grace-based parents realize that their children need security in their hearts, significance in their lives, and strength for the future. They also know that these things don't come via prepackaged programs based on clever formulas. These things come by way of the heart—transferred through parents who enjoy a grace relationship with Christ.

> Grace-based parents realize that their children need security in their hearts, significance in their lives, and strength for the future.

I'm reviewing this information for two reasons. The first is because I'm hoping this view of grace will become a template for the way you think as a mom or dad. Grace-based parenting is not a checklist for parenting; it's a lifestyle. It's a clear attempt to retrofit your minds to respond to your children in the same way God responds to you. Being different, vulnerable, and candid isn't something you *do* as a grace-based family; it's something you *are*.

The second reason for this review is to remind you of how much you have to lose when you fail to provide the next key ingredient of grace-based parenting. That's what this chapter is about. *The fourth characteristic of grace-based homes is this: They are homes that give children the freedom to make mistakes.*

THE WAGES OF SIN

You run a risk any time you talk about sin and grace in the same sentence. People assume you're trying to set up a nice little theological system allows you to do whatever you want. That's not what the Bible says grace is. Grace can be used in a specific sense, which is as a gift of forgiveness that you don't deserve. Grace can also be used in a general sense, which is as the freedom and latitude that God allows you as you develop a more intimate relationship with Him. I'm talking about a lifestyle and a set of choices that are the outgrowth of your walk with Him.

Let me assure you that just phrasing it this way gives some people all the ammunition they need to use my own words against me. Grace scares a lot of people because it doesn't come with enough bullet points and three-part outlines for those who would rather not have to think too much. Grace demands that you actually *walk* by faith. That's why I'm confident many would assume that when it comes to sin, grace offers too much latitude. They say, "See, this grace-based parenting thing is just a smoke screen for making up the rules to live so that you can accommodate your own vices. It's nothing but a license to sin." Sorry, Charlie. I'd have to rip Romans chapters 5 through 8 out of my Bible in order to believe such nonsense. There is nothing in the realm of grace that gives anyone the license to ignore God's standards.

If anything, grace should motivate you to a higher holiness. Grace-based homes aren't places where family members assume they can say whatever they want, see whatever they want, hear whatever they want, taste or drink whatever they want, or touch whatever they want. That's not grace. That's someone wanting to live his or her own life with no regard for what God has said or what He thinks. But when grace is in place, there is clearly a different attitude toward sin than in homes without grace. If I could summarize grace in one sentence, it would be something like this: "As long as you are pleasing God, you're pretty much free to do whatever you want." But keep in mind that "pleasing" God is contingent on our faith in Him, not on our ability to maintain a righteous and moral standard, as so many assume. Hebrews 11:6 says that "without faith it is impossible to please God." People who walk by faith are far more capable of developing a godly and righteous lifestyle because they are finding their power for living in their personal relationship with the Lord. That's why the Scriptures say, "The righteous will live by faith" (Romans 1:17; Galatians 3:11).

Legalistic families are a night-and-day contrast to grace-based families. Legalistic parents maintain a relationship with God through obedience to a standard. The goal of all this when it comes to their children is to keep sin from getting into their home. They do their best to create an environment that controls as many of the avenues as possible that sin could use to work its way into the inner sanctum. They teach the standards and rules that God outlines in the Scriptures and do everything within their power to keep their children from choosing sin. In these types of families, it's real easy for kids to assume that *things* can actually be sin (R-rated movies, spiked hair, short skirts, kids who hang out in groups at the mall, rap music, etc.). These types of homes also make it easy to assume that certain *actions* are inherently sinful (dancing, watching *The Simpsons*, coed swimming, going to secular rock concerts, French kissing, etc.). If the list gets long enough, and the barriers that protect the children from these evil "things" and sinful "actions" stay strong enough, it is assumed that the children will find it easier to maintain holiness. This style of parenting might dictate where the family lives, who the children's friends are, how the kids are educated, and what type of youth group they belong to.

When these children do sin, they are punished more for allowing the sin to *happen* than they are for the fact that it happened. It's as though the power to sin or not to sin was somehow connected to their personal will power and resolve. Guilt and fear can plague children in these homes without the children ever falling into sin. They can get fearful when they simply get in proximity to one of those "things" that is considered sinful (see above). They can even feel guilty if they sense a twinge of inclination toward one of the "actions" that personify sin. This forces them to pull away from the people who live in the mainstream of life. They sometimes even become skeptical and selective regarding the other legalistic people within their safe environment. These families are preoccupied with keeping sin out by putting a fence between them and the world.

The difference with grace-based families is that they don't bother spending much time putting fences up because they know full well that sin is already present and accounted for inside their family. To these types of parents, sin is not an *action* or an *object* that penetrates their defenses; it is a preexisting condition that permeates their being. The graceless home requires kids to be good and gets angry and punishes them when they are bad. The grace-based home assumes kids will struggle with sin and helps them learn how to tap into God's power to help them get stronger.

It's not that grace-based homes don't take their children's sin seriously. Nor is it that grace-based homes circumvent consequences. It isn't even that grace-based homes do nothing to protect their children from attacks and temptations that threaten them from the outside. They do all these things, but not for the same reasons. Grace-based homes aren't trusting in the moral safety of their home or the spiritual environment they've created to empower their children to resist sin. They know that ultimately a home and an environment are no match against the forces of evil. When their children do sin, grace-based parents don't get surprised. They expect it. They assume that sin is an ongoing dilemma that their children must constantly contend with.

This attitude changes their mind-set about finding victory. The freedom children enjoy in a grace-based family is this: They are accepted as sinners who desire to become more like Christ rather than be seen as nice Christian kids trying to maintain a good moral code. Grace is committed to bringing children up from their sin; legalism puts them on a high standard and works overtime to keep them from falling down.

> Grace understands that the only real solution for our children's sin is the work of Christ on their behalf.

Grace understands that the only *real* solution for our children's sin is the work of Christ on their behalf. It is not pristine spiritual conditions or their good behavior. Grace realizes that there is *nothing* any of us can do on our own to improve our chances with God. There is *nothing* any of us can do on our own to gain more of God's love. There is *nothing* any of us can do on our own to gain victory over our sin. The only thing any one of us has going for us is Jesus.

EXOSKELETONS AND ENDOSKELETONS

Legalism uses outside forces to help children maintain their moral walk. Their strength is based on the *environment* they live in. Another way to think of this is to consider a crustacean. A lobster's skeleton surrounds him and holds him in. In the same way, legalism depends on a controlled environment to hold children's urges in place and the temptations away. Grace, on the other hand, sees the strength of children by what is inside them—more specifically, Who is inside them. The unlimited power of Christ and the thorough effect of His finished work on the cross form the internal belief system that functions as the skeleton that helps to keep them standing strong.

Keeping with this analogy, when we take a sharp blow to our human bodies, we may break a bone. In most cases we can set the broken bone in a cast until it becomes strong again. If the bone in this analogy represents our children's belief system and the break represents a sin problem they have, there are numerous things we have to turn to (not the least of which are consequences and discipline) that can help them get spiritually strong again. It doesn't work this way when the children's source of strength over their sin and temptation is some external environment, a newfangled program, or a bunch of rules. If there is a breach of any of these things, the children's power is gone. Another way of saying it would be: If you break a person's arm, he's got a broken arm. If you split open a lobster's external covering, it's dead.

It's almost a cliché because it happens so often—kids raised in strict and safe Christian environments who go off to college and become party animals living wild, out-of-control lives. They might even become promiscuous. They seem powerless to resist any of the negative options coming at them (which is because they *are* powerless). It's not that children in legalistic Christian homes (or fear-based Christian families) don't have Christ in their lives; it's just that they haven't been taught how to appropriate His power to overcome the spiritual challenges they encounter. They have been taught that their power over sin and their victory over temptation rest in things other than Christ. Unfortunately, the Bible doesn't back up that premise. There is no power outside Christ; there is only the illusion of it.

Grace-based parenting, on the other hand, can send kids off to college less inclined toward the vices that surround them. This has more to do with the perspective these parents had throughout their children's early lives. Whereas legalism seeks to keep children from becoming partiers, grace assumes they were born that way. Whereas legalism seeks to keep children from being promiscuous, grace assumes they grow into adolescence with a growing desire to become physical with someone of the opposite sex.

Your children's propensity toward sin shouldn't surprise you; it shouldn't threaten you; and it shouldn't even really *bother* you. You know you've given birth to sinners, children just like the parents who sired them. You realize that your children have a bent toward selfishness, stubbornness, and lawlessness—exactly the kind of people Christ loves and for whom He died. By acknowledging your children's bent toward sin from the outset, you can encourage your children to struggle with their sin out in the open where you can talk about it and direct them to the power of Christ. And when the children are actually sinning, grace makes it easy for you to have open, candid, and vulnerable discussions about these areas where they struggle. Your children will be able to talk with you about their internal battles with jealousy, lust, greed, or anger.

You should be able to talk openly and honestly about sin because you're so aware that you and your spouse are sinners, too. King David said, "If you, O Lord, kept a record of sins, O Lord, who could stand? But with you there is forgiveness; therefore you are feared" (Psalm 130:3–4). Grace demands a humility and sensitivity toward your children's battles with sin because grace is a daily reminder of how desperately you need the Savior as well. You should join David in thanking God that He doesn't keep score when it comes to your sin.

It makes it a lot easier for children to deal with their sin when you don't make them feel ashamed for even having a struggle. You know your children struggle and want to be part of the dialogue that helps them look for power at the foot of the cross.

You realize that Christ didn't die for you because you had good qualities that were worth saving. He died for you because you had bad qualities that left you without a prayer. When you understand this, you can use your grace-based environment to extend a graciousness toward your children when they struggle with sin in their lives. When a child sins, grace doesn't ask, "What's wrong with you?" It knows what's wrong. It doesn't ask, "Why did you do something stupid like that?" It knows why they did something stupid. It's not bent on pointing out the shortcomings of children, but rather it is excited about pointing children toward the unconditional love of Jesus Christ.

Paul had a famous discussion with himself in Romans chapter 7. In this passage he went back and forth about his desire to do the right thing, but his tendency was to do the wrong thing. Listen to how he put it:

> I do not understand what I do. For what I want to do I do not do, but what I hate I do . . . For I have the desire to do what is good, but I cannot carry it out. For what I do is not the good I want to do; no, the evil I do not want to do—this I keep on doing. Now if I do what I do not want to do, it is no longer I who do it, but it is sin living in me that does it . . . What a wretched man I am! Who will rescue me from this body of death? Thanks be to God—through Jesus Christ our Lord! (Romans 7:15, 18b–20, 24–25)

Paul had an absolute grasp of the grace of God. He understood that he walked on very fragile feet of clay. He was extremely aware of the wicked capabilities that lurked within his own heart. He didn't beat himself up for being this way; instead, he rejoiced that Christ loved him in spite of it—loved him so much, in fact, that He died to give him the power to win his battle over his sin.

In the book of Colossians, Paul wets the ink on his quill and goes after (in grace) those who would want to create regulations and human behavior systems as a hedge against sin. Listen:

So then, just as you received Christ Jesus as Lord, continue to live in him, rooted and built up in him, strengthened in the faith as you were taught, and overflowing with thankfulness. See to it that no one takes you captive through hollow and deceptive philosophy, which depends on human tradition and the basic principles of this world rather than on Christ. For in Christ all the fullness of the Deity lives in bodily form, and you have been given fullness in Christ, who is the head over every power and authority . . . Since you died with Christ to the basic principles of this world, why, as though you still belonged to it, do you submit to its rules: "Do not handle! Do not taste! Do not touch!"? These are all destined to perish with use, because they are based on human commands and teachings. Such regulations indeed have an appearance of wisdom, with their self-imposed worship, their false humility and their harsh treatment of the body, but they lack any value in restraining sensual indulgence . . . Since, then, you have been raised with Christ, set your hearts on things above, where Christ is seated at the right hand of God. Set your minds on things above, not on earthly things. For you died, and your life is now hidden with Christ in God. (Colossians 2:6–10, 20–23; 3:1–3).

Bottom line: Grace-based families realize that their children will struggle with sin. They consider it an honor to be used by God to show their children how to find true forgiveness in Christ. They are not intimidated by the dialogue that brings the discussion of sin into the light. In fact, they are grateful to be able to come alongside their children with an unconditional love during some of their toughest hours.

WINNING WITH LOVE AND CONSEQUENCES

To help you provide a home where children are free to make mistakes, you should follow a proven plan that helps you respond when they actually fall and fail. Let's look at some do's and don'ts.

1. Your Response

The keyword is *response,* as opposed to *react.* When your children sin, it is easy to let them have it with both barrels. Whether it's a lie, socking a sibling, or getting caught cheating on a test at school, your natural inclination is to light into them with a vengeance for letting you down, embarrassing you, or causing you stress. This is how many parents react—parents who don't understand the nature of the sin as a condition of the human heart.

A grace response to your children's sin is to avoid condemnation. You can evaluate their wrong actions, discuss their negative effects, and even voice the pain and disappointment that you have experienced as a result of it. But you don't want to condemn. Condemnation corners them and doesn't offer much hope. Condemnation attacks their character rather than addresses their behavior. When you condemn, it causes a reflex within them to defend themselves. Often your condemnation does little more than make a bad situation far worse.

Instead, if you make a commitment to walk them through their mistake with love and grace, they are more inclined to adopt a humble attitude, experience remorse, and express a desire to ask for forgiveness. This attitude from you will more likely motivate them to want to trust Christ to help them achieve victory over this particular sin in the future.

2. Consequences

One of the most ungraceful things you can do is to circumvent the consequences of your children's sin. Children learn from discipline and have an internal sense of justice that needs to know they have paid their debt for their infraction and can move on with their lives. When you either let your children get away with their sin or promise them consequences but fail to deliver, you upset the scales of justice that tip within their souls.

Two incidents involving our own children illustrate this. Our youngest son, Colt, had done something that caused him to lose the privilege of watching television for two weekends in a row. It was a punishment that had been meted out by my wife. She had mentioned it to me but by the second week, frankly, it had slipped my mind. On that Saturday afternoon, I had rented a movie and asked Colt if he wanted to sit down and watch it with me. That's when he informed me that he couldn't, reminding me that he was in the final weekend of his consequences.

The second incident was years ago, when our oldest daughter, Karis, was a little girl. Darcy had taken her to the grocery store. While there, Karis acted up and disobeyed her mother, which many kids do. Darcy told her that because of her actions, she would be disciplined when they got home. But mom and daughter didn't get home for another two hours. Because we live in the Arizona desert, Darcy needed to get the groceries out of the stifling heat of the garage and into the house as soon as possible. It took more than a few minutes for Darcy to haul all the groceries from the car to the kitchen. She was in the process of putting things in the freezer when Karis reminded her that she was supposed to get punished.

"Can I please have my punishment now so that I can get it over with and go out and play?" Karis asked.

In each scenario, the children responded to their internal sense of justice. They wanted to get their punishment over with so that they could pay their debt in full and move on with their lives.

If you manipulate the situation to get your kids off the hook for some sin that they committed or you minimize the punishment to something far less than they deserve, you only set up your children to do things that are much worse. Believe me, if you've ever been around a juvenile detention center, this is a recurring theme. Mom or Dad kept pulling strings, buying them out of trouble, or simply allowing them to get away with it. The next time, they tried something far worse. Providing consequences for sin *is* a loving form of grace. It says, "I love you too much to let you continue in this pattern and grow up to be bad." Meting out fair and consistent consequences for their negative actions tells children there is a mature and decent parent overseeing their lives. Letting them get away with sin says just the opposite. It tells them they have an immature parent who is more concerned about their comfort than with their children's dignity.

Some mistakes have natural consequences: school detention, paying for something they broke, public or personal apologies, police arrest, or facing the judge. Depending on the circumstances, natural consequences might also be reinforced with additional discipline from the parent. For instance, let's say your teenager got a speeding ticket. Besides having to pay the ticket, go to driver's rehabilitation school, or pay the extra premium on his auto insurance, you may also choose to take away his driving privileges for a period of time.

3. Prodigals

Some children age you quickly. They reject your love, your leadership, and your discipline. These are children whose hearts may be cold toward God and colder toward you. There are a couple of things to keep in mind when you're dealing with prodigals.

First, resist the urge to beat yourself up. When children fall into the underworld of drugs, alcohol, sex, or crime, don't second-guess yourself trying to figure out what you did wrong to cause your child to run so fast and stray so far. A serious case of objectivity is needed here. All parents make mistakes. Besides this, some children are hell-bent on rebelling, and there's nothing you can do to change that. Sometimes their behavior isn't an issue between you and them—it's an issue between them and God.

Speaking of God, He has a word of encouragement for you about this whole "beating yourself up" thing. Luke chapter 15 contains the classic prodigal son story. When you step back and look at the greater point Jesus was making, it's obvious that He used this story to describe how some of God's children rebel toward Him. One of the take-home applications for parents of prodigals comes from a logical deduction of the story. If the father in the story represents God, and the boy who runs off to a foreign land represents one of God's rebellious children, then it is obvious that God is telling us, "Listen, I'm God, and yet because of free will, I can't (or won't) stop My children from rebelling.

If I can't keep My children in line, and I'm God, I don't see why you should be beating yourself up for not keeping yours in line."

There are several other key points we can learn from the story of the prodigal son:

Second point: Don't give up on them. God doesn't. Prodigals may hurt you deeply. They may bring huge embarrassment to you. But don't give up on them.

Third point: Don't accommodate or bankroll their rebellion. Let them figure out how to finance it. For the most part, rebellion is expensive, and sin makes most people stupid. If you don't finance their prodigal experiences, it will bring them to the end of their options more quickly.

Fourth point: Be prepared to forgive them if and when they finally repent. Forgiveness doesn't mean that there aren't consequences for actions, nor does it restore trust, but it does impart value and begins rebuilding the relationship.

Fifth point: Resist the urge to replay the hurt they've put you through. If they repent, kill the fatted calf, have a party, and move on. Reminding them of how much pain they've cost you is counter-productive to the situation.

4. Discipline

The key thing about grace-based parenting is that God gives you variety in how you discipline your children. There are those who believe that there is only one method of discipline the Bible suggests for young children—spanking. Yet God uses myriad ways to discipline His own children in the Bible. He's a God who's never made two sunsets alike. He's an original God. He allows you to choose the method of discipline that best matches your child's temperament and personality. Some people rely on corporal discipline, assuming that works effectively every time. We have a son who could look corporal discipline in the eye and not flinch. We found other methods far more effective at getting his attention and helping him learn from his mistakes. We have a daughter, on the other hand, who would start crying *before* the first swat on her behind.

You may have an unfortunate history when it comes to discipline. Because of what you went through, either you don't trust yourself or you have such discomfort using that method because it was improperly used on you. Remember, you have a God of grace who gives you grace to work through the methods of discipline that are most effective and align well with you.

we all make mistakes

Porch lights. They mark the night with their white-yellow glow. Some beckon. Some warn. Some burn to protect those on the inside from the shadows that lurk on the edges of the darkness.

For some, their porch lights shine like the star of hope against a cobalt sky. They bathe the night with their light and wash the sleeping home with quiet. All is well. All is bright.

There are a handful of porch lights that will never go out. They can't. They went on one evening when that son or daughter stormed out into the thickness and blackness of the cold. The door slammed. The feet pounded across the wooden planks of the porch and then disappeared beyond the light's half circle.

It's been a long time. For some, months. Others, years. There are a few who have put a decade of running between them and that porch light. The prayers on the inside haven't stopped. The hope might have fainted and faltered a few times, but it's still there.

That's why the light still burns . . . and will keep burning. It's a God thing. It's a Redeemer thing. Grace-based homes are not homes without sin or regrets. They are just homes where, no matter what, you can't be written off. They are homes where young and restless hearts are free to be different, vulnerable, and candid. They're allowed to make mistakes. Huge ones sometimes. But because grace is inside, the front porch light will always glow outside.

Regardless of why they left, they can always come back. Regardless of where they went, they can always come home. And regardless of what they did, they can always come in.

CHAPTER 11

Evening Grace

Why *grace?*

Of all the adjectives I could choose to qualify the kind of parenting we are to do, why did I choose this one?

After all, the list of adjectives is endless. Several that come to mind could have made a nice first impression on a book cover:

Bold Parenting

Smart Parenting

Savvy Parenting

Tough Parenting

But these wouldn't have been good book titles. They don't capture God's heart. They don't even come close. They reflect only our hearts, and as such, they don't do that very well. Among other things, these titles are way too confining and a little too inviting.

Because of the stewardship you have been given as parents, you need a phrase that conveys a far greater vision for your children.

There is only one phrase that works—*grace-based parenting*. This phrase captures the heart of God in an all-encompassing way. Grace includes His love, embraces His mercy, and honors His sacrifice.

Grace is an amazing adjective because it's an amazing grace. The whole world knows about it, even sings about it. People love the sound of this word because they need the *point* of it. Without grace, you don't have a chance. Without grace, you can't find your way. Without grace, you wouldn't matter.

God wrapped up His whole wonderful plan for us in this single, simple word. Grace sings out, "Joy to the world." It calls out, "Come unto Me." It cries out, "It is finished!"

And so, it seemed only fitting that when I needed to find a word that would summarize the heart of God and meet the criteria of our greatest calling, it would be "grace."

You have been singled out to do a favor for God. He is asking you to be His representative to a small but vital part of the next generation. He needs someone to be His voice, His arms, and His heart. He chose you.

He chose you to assist Him in a miracle. He gave you children and then said, "Now go, and give these precious lives *meaning*." It's a mandate that comes with a great reward if you succeed, but a heavy price if you fail.

This is where many parents panic. When they realize that their job is to raise up children to love and serve God, they wonder how on earth they will do that.

The answer isn't on earth. It's found in heaven. It's sitting on an eternal throne. He has many names, but among my favorites is "The God of Grace." You wonder, *How am I to raise up children to love and serve God?* The answer is actually not that difficult. You simply need to treat your children the way God treats you.

He does it in His grace.

And here's the good part. If the only thing you get right as parents is His grace, everything else will be just fine.

I can vouch for that. I didn't have a lot going for me when I became a father. My role model was average, my experience was limited, and my talent was suspect. I made a ton of mistakes. I've left things out and put things in that didn't belong. But there has been one goal that Darcy and I have focused on from the beginning. We wanted to make sure that to the best of our ability, we raised our children in an environment of grace.

The result is that we have seen what God promises is true, and His grace *is* sufficient.

Yet I suppose some would say that the jury is still out on how we did. And I guess if that's the way you keep score, the jury will remain out until the last one of our children is married and has children.

But every once in a while, something happens that is like a love note from God that says, "You chose the right path in how you raised your kids." Sometimes grace was *all* we had to offer them, but we have figured out that if grace is all we've got, grace is all we need.

We have four children. Our second-born is a son named Cody. One evening, during the winter quarter of his high-school senior year, Cody, who was eighteen years old at the time, had a brief conversation with me before he said "Good night" and retired to bed. I was working at my computer and had assumed he had gone to sleep. But something prompted him to sit down at his desk and write a poem. Twenty-five minutes after I said good night to him, he came back out to read me what he had written. His poetic effort gave me reason to hope.

MY GOD Remans
By Cody Kimmel

When all that ought to be is gone
And freedom falls to feeling
And all that life's been born to own
Gets lost in my soul's stealing
When every color fades to gray
And love seems but a stain
And fleshly hope is thrown away
Indeed, my God remains.

When clouds form scenes of good times past
And every road not traveled
And all great things that never last
And every goal unraveled
When thunder drowns the voice of truth
And lies become my bane
I cry to God in my reckless youth,
And yes, He still remains.

When birthdays seem like one more day
And winter crowns my brow
When years long gone start to betray
My body years from now;
When Death sneaks slowly to my bed
And robs me of my pain,
My soul will bless the day I said,
"Thank God, my God remains."[1]

notes

Chapter 1: Why Well-Meaning Parenting Falls Short

1. Check out Philippians 2:12–16 for the full context. This is an excellent goal for grace-based parenting. Notice that it follows the powerful *kenosis* (Greek for "to empty") passage where Christ "emptied" Himself of all His divine privileges (not His divinity) and humbled Himself in order to reach out to sinful men.
2. John Fischer, *Fearless Faith* (Eugene, OR: Harvest House, 2002), 21–31.
3. I wrote an entire book on the subject of high control. You might want to look at it more closely. It's titled *How to Deal With Powerful Personalities* (Colorado Springs: Focus on the Family, 1994) and is available at www.familymatters.net.
4. I'm indebted to the excellent chart by Max Lucado in his book *In the Grip of Grace* (Dallas: Word Publishing, 1996), 8–9.
5. Ibid.
6. 2 Corinthians 5:21.
7. 2 Corinthians 12:9.
8. Hebrews 4:15–16.
9. Proverbs 22:6.

Chapter 2: The Truth Behind Grace

1. C. S. Lewis: Cited in Scott Hoezee, *The Riddle of Grace* (Grand Rapids: Eerdmans, 1996), 42.

2. *Young's Analytical Concordance to the Bible* (Grand Rapids: Eerdmans, 1972), 783.

3. Ibid.

4. Randy Alcorn, *The Grace and Truth Paradox* (Sisters, OR: Multnomah, 2002), 37.

5. Philip Yancey, *What's So Amazing About Grace?* (Grand Rapids: Zondervan, 1997), 195.

Chapter 3: A Secure Love

1. See Genesis 1:26–27.

2. Family secrets are always toxic. The deception and lack of forthrightness that is required to keep them from the people closest to you is always felt in their hearts. When family secrets finally come out later in life, the child is forced to wonder what else has been a deception. Truth sets people free. Children can process truth a lot younger than they can endure deception. The sooner the truth is out in the open, the better. Once the facts are on the table, they can no longer haunt.

Chapter 4: A Significant Purpose

1. Revelation 1:1–3.

2. Genesis 1:26–27.

3. Robert Lewis, *Raising a Modern-Day Knight* (Colorado Springs: Focus on the Family, 1997), 83.

4. Hollywood Pictures, *Mr. Holland's Opus.*

5. Proverbs 9:10.

6. Allan Bloom, *The Closing of the American Mind* (New York: Simon & Schuster, 1982), 27.

7. Reuben Welch, *We Really Do Need Each Other* (Nashville, TN: Generoux Nelson, 1973), 92.

8. "Gonna Serve Somebody" by Bob Dylan © Special Rider Music ℗ 1979 CBS Inc. Used by permission.

9. Matthew 10:30.

10. *October Sky* quote and permission.

Chapter 5: A Strong Hope

1. Acts 9:1–19a.

2. See the excellent work of Chuck Swindoll, *The Strong Family* (Portland, OR: Multnomah, 1991), 59–78.

3. If you want further help in achieving this tall order, you might want to read the book I wrote on this very subject: Tim Kimmel, *Raising Kids Who Turn Out Right* (Phoenix: Family Matters, 1993). Available at www.familymatters.net.

4. This is the lesson the children learned regarding Jesus in *The Lion, the Witch and the Wardrobe* by C. S. Lewis. In this classic children's story, Aslan the lion is the character that represents Christ. The children learned that Aslan was not safe, but he was good.

5. For an excellent exhortation on this, read the greater context of 2 Corinthians 4:16–18.

6. Genesis 1:4, 10, 12, 18, 21, 25, 31.

7. Revelation 1:8; 22:13.

Chapter 7: The Freedom to Be Different

1. *The Nelson Study Bible*, (Nashville: Thomas Nelson Publishers, 1997), 2142.

Chapter 8: The Freedom to Be Vulnerable

1. Matthew 27:44.
2. His half brothers James and Jude would not only make key contributions to the New Testament canon, but they would both play demanding roles in the establishment of the church. James especially had his hands full in his responsibilities as overseer of the church in Jerusalem.

Chapter 9: The Freedom to Be Candid

1. Dan B. Allender, *The Wounded Heart* (Colorado Springs: NavPress, 1991), 183.

Chapter 11: Evening Grace

1. "My God Remains." Copyright 2003 by Cody Kimmel. Used by permission.

Special Preview of
Tim Kimmel's Next Book

Why Christian Kids Rebel

Trading Heartache for Hope

AVAILABLE OCTOBER 2004

CHAPTER ONE

When So Many Do So Little with So Much

Martin sat alone at his son's desk. With his face buried in his hands, he fought conflicting inner urges to either explode in anger or implode into the sense of helplessness churning in his soul. The visit to his son's dormitory was unannounced. The boy's roommate was nice enough to let him wait in the room until his son returned from class. They had exchanged the awkward obligatory small talk for a few minutes before the roommate came up with some reason to leave. In the privacy of his son's dorm room, Martin had enough time to validate what he had feared.

The alarms had actually started going off in his and his wife's heart when their son had come home for Christmas break. For a kid who had left home with a faith forged in a serious Christian family, there seemed to be little evidence of it when he arrived back home at the end of his first semester. They had assumed he would change a little while at college, but they never figured he would change this much. During Christmas break, they found a boy who had no interest in calling or connecting with any of the Christian friends he had been so close to before. He developed a deliberate glazed-over look the few times they had mentioned anything about God or church. But what really scared them was how he had stayed out past 3:00 A.M. most nights. One night he didn't come home until the next afternoon. He offered no explanation for where he had been and got belligerent with his mother when she inquired.

And now here, in this tiny room that served as a microcosm of his son's value system, Martin could see evidence of a boy who was heading down a road that beared no similarity to the one his parents had encouraged him to take. The woman on the screen saver of his son's computer wouldn't even fall into the "soft-core" category of pornography. She was probably scanned from one of the pictures in the stack of *Hustler* and *Penthouse* magazines on his nightstand next to a half empty box of condoms. The supposedly virgin son they had off to college had been busy. He'd taken up drinking, too. The stack of cans that covered half of the window wasn't just dorm room decoration. There was enough smoke in the room to indicate that a fire was burning in his boy's soul. But it wasn't the fire of spiritual passion anymore.

Martin had seen this same thing happen to a couple of his friends' children. He had heard the excuses they made and the blame they passed around. They put the responsibility at the feet of the universities. In one case, it seemed like such an ironic accusation since the child (in this case, a daughter) had gone to a "Christian" university. Some of Martin's friends had felt the lack of adequate programming in their church during their children's teenage years was the reason they had fallen away from their spiritual moorings. But Martin felt there were three people responsible for what was happening. One was somewhere in a class across campus, the other was back home waiting for Martin to call and give her a report, and the last was sitting in his son's dorm room wondering where he'd gone wrong.

The principal stood in the hallway as the three young men passed by— two juniors and a sophomore. They wore the uniform of the Christian school, and a look on their report cards would reveal that they had given all the correct biblical answers and theological responses to the tests they had taken over the years. One of them had even represented the school at a Bible memory competition, bringing home a huge trophy that stood in the glass case at the entrance to the gymnasium.

But as he watched these three students stroll by, the question "What's wrong with this picture?" kept running through his head. These three young men may have known all the answers to the Christian belief system his school taught, but there was nothing about them that reflected any sense of appreciation for what Jesus had done for them on a cross. They were dead center in the social and academic life of a Christian school each day, but their attitudes and actions reflected that they were walking contradictions of the school's values. There were no signs of genuine hearts for God—just a bunch of cliché answers that had been drilled into their heads.

He knew how much they teased and mocked the handful of students who were serious about their faith in God. The mannerisms and actions of this trio reflected the "worldly" thinking that their parents had put them in the Christian school to avoid. Outside the school they lived and acted like reckless kids with no hope. They made trouble in their youth group at church. Their hard stares dared the young, enthusiastic youth pastor to teach them something they didn't already know. Their clothes, shoes, and overall styles outside the school showed how conscious they were about wearing the right labels. But the one label that mattered the most was one they seemed to spurn. They talked and acted like kids who had zero desire to please God. The principal knew that in spite of all these three boys knew about God, their words and actions were evidence of where their heart was. *What a shame*, he thought, *Their parents have tried so hard and paid so much, and all they are getting back are three boys who could care less.*

These three had been given so much but had embraced so little. They had their faith spoon fed to them, but all their parents and this Christian school got in return were spoiled, indulged, Christian kids. What really messed up the picture was the fact that these kids came from what most would call good, conscientious Christian families.

As the principal watched them disappear around the corner, he wondered whether the word *Christian* was little more than an adjective in their life—a bunch of biblical clichés and spiritually-canned behavior.

HEADACHES AND HEARTACHES

Few things grieve a Christian parent's heart more than a child who is heading down a self-destructive path. Most of the time these young people are closed to any sense of reasoning by you as a parent. Sometimes they are even closed to talking at all. They won't let you inside thier words enough to get a glimpse of the contradictions that are tormenting them. When they finally do speak up, you hear philosophies of life that bear no kin to the one you thought you gave them. And what really hurts is that most of the time it's a 180° turn from the direction they were heading throughout most of their childhood. It's as though the cherubs who sat on your lap and basked in the Bible stories you read to them when they were little suddenly enrolled in Saddam Hussein Junior High.

God ticks them off, you tick them off, and life ticks them off. They are capable of being stubborn, obstinate, argumentative, aloof, and moody. They often seem embarrassed by your outward commitment to God and indifferent to your spiritual advice. These are kids who have no problem following through on a series of dumb decisions that get them into trouble.

Some Christian kids' rebellion is a short-lived parenthesis of stupidity that they come out of rather quickly. It's just a brief little jaunt through the "childhood from Hell," and then they're over it. But a more serious brand of rebellion has the potential of wrecking a child's view of God indefinitely. And as serious as that is, it's only the beginning of many things that can have a long-term negative effect on them. This kind of toxic rebellion can set children up for relationship nightmares that dog them the rest of their lives.

And then there's the textbook Christian kid who goes through all the right motions, learns all the right truths, makes all the right choices, and appears to be a great candidate for being a good

Christian parent, but never feels inclined to make a difference once he or she is an adult. The fact is, rebellion isn't always outward and hostile. Sometimes it's a lack of passion, a lack of concern, or a lack of motivation by someone who has been raised in a spiritual greenhouse. They've heard the truth and accepted it. They've learned the principles and believed them. They've seen God work in many miraculous ways and enjoyed it. They just haven't invested these gifts from God into a life that will shine for Him. They grow up to be people who go to church when it's convenient, serving reluctantly, tipping God with the leftovers of their money. They remain mute about their beliefs, go for months or even years on end without deliberately studying their Bible, and never graduate from an elementary understanding of what they believe.

Rebellion doesn't always have to be ugly; sometimes it's just lazy.

It's also contagious. Everybody knows that "sins of the father" thing in the Bible, you know, that curse of our parents' sin that comes back to haunt the third and fourth generation of off-spring. But that's only about parents who deliberately *hate* God. It's not talking about the ones who simply struggle living out their faith. Besides, it's a curse that can be pre-empted by the Holy Spirit simply by asking. Some kids' rebellion might be rooted in this. But sometimes it's the "sins of the youth group" or the "sins of the Christian school group" or the "sins of the peer group" that get ahold of our children's original faith. None of these *groups* are responsible for the individual choices our children make, but because so much of a child's life is *reflective* rather than *original,* our kids are more inclined to model the attitude of the people they gravitate to, rather than the force that fuels their faith.

Active or passive rebellion. Defiance or indifference. Both net the same results. There is no advancement of the kingdom of heaven coming from the choices these rebellious Christian kids are making. Over the years, I have known a lot of young people who have been given great spiritual assets, but did so little with them. And over these same years my heart has grown more and more saddened by what I see happening in our mainline Christian homes. I see parents who genuinely love God, and obviously love their children, going to sacrificial lengths to ensure their children an almost "country club" Christian experience.

Parents surround their children with all the wonderful books, videos, and programs designed to galvanize their heart for God during the infant/toddler years. They sacrifice to put them in Christian schools or make an even greater sacrifice to home-school them. If they put their children in public school, the parents carefully monitor what the children are receiving and work overtime to augment and offset areas where there is a deficit. They send them through wonderful Christian camping experiences and do everything they can to ensure them a tremendous church experience. In spite of it all, some children choose to rebel. I've seen blatant rebellion coming from all educational options, all youth group options, and all church options. To assume that any of the parental options I've just listed will somehow help you avoid having children who rebel is a naiveté that will almost guarantee that your child will rebel.

That's because Christianity isn't something we do; it's something we are.

GRACE-BASED PARENTING AND REBELLION

Depending on where you are, you might feel like a failure. You either have kids who are steeped in rebellion against you and God, or you're fairly sure you have one or two heading that way. Perhaps you have friends who, by all appearances, have done everything right. Yet they have kids who have rejected their faith, who have made personal choices that contradict the precious things their parents stand for. If you're like everyone else, you want some assurance that if you do everything the way it is to be done, certain results should be a given. As you've seen by reading *Grace-Based Parenting*, raising spiritually passionate kids who have a strong belief system is not formulaic. You have to deal with a child's abstract emotions and fickle heart. Your children's relationships with God can't simply be programmed by their environment, as a result of receiving a Christian education, or because you had regular family devotions.

However, lest you say, "What's the point? If things aren't going to turn out right regardless of what we do as parents, why put so much effort into the spiritual side of parenting?" please know that there is hope. There are things that we can do and not do that will allow our children to get a clearer, more attractive opportunity to embrace our faith and live out the values they've been taught at home. Knowing what these things are will either be preventative or prescriptive when it comes to their making the choice to rebel against God. That's why I'm writing this book. I want to:

- Show you how to release yourself from the bondage of checklist Christian parenting.

- Free you to allow your children to struggle as they finalize their faith.

- Help you develop a strong heart-to-heart relationship with your child, especially in those times when he or she is running from God.

- Show you how to launch your children into the future with a faith that clearly belongs to them.

- Teach you how to raise kids who are willing to make a positive spiritual difference in the world.

- Take the fear out of the corridor of time your children spend being "prodigal" sons and daughters.

- Raise the odds that all the hard work you've put into developing your child's relationship with God pays off.

- Help protect you from the heartache a rebellious teenager can bring to your entire family.

- Help you raise kids who are prepared to transfer the family values you've embraced to the next generation.

- Show you how to avoid the many pitfalls inherent in raising children inside a spiritual environment.

That last bullet point might have caught you by surprise. You may never have thought that the things you are trying to do right might be the very things that trigger your children into rebellion against you and against God. What's sad is that some conventional wisdom about how to raise Christian kids actually baits them into rebellion. The naive, well-intended parent follows the checklist only to find their son or daughter in spiritual indifference. And as you may have heard, indifference is the true opposite of love. It stands in contrast with all you've done and the environment you've provided.

IT'S A MARATHON, NOT A SPRINT

Whether your kids are barely walking, too young to drive, or too old to "ground," you can gain some calm in the midst of their spiritual calamity. Having kids in your Christian home who rebel is never fun. It's often a deep and desperate hurt. But there is help and hope. There might even be something to look forward to. Understanding why they rebel, and having a working knowledge of not only the drawbacks that lead them to rebel but the countermeasures that can minimize these drawbacks can be worth the trip through the outer banks of hell you're in. You might feel that your child's rebellion is like running a marathon that has no finish line. But then again, you might be surprised by what is waiting for you if you don't give up.

When I was a child, I talked like a child, I thought like a child, I reasoned like a child. When I became a man, I put away childish ways.

1 Corinthians 13:11